I0439798

THE RISE OF ISIL: IRAQ AND BEYOND

JOINT HEARING

BEFORE THE

SUBCOMMITTEE ON TERRORISM, NONPROLIFERATION, AND TRADE

AND THE

SUBCOMMITTEE ON THE MIDDLE EAST AND NORTH AFRICA

OF THE

COMMITTEE ON FOREIGN AFFAIRS HOUSE OF REPRESENTATIVES

ONE HUNDRED THIRTEENTH CONGRESS

SECOND SESSION

JULY 15, 2014

Serial No. 113–215

Printed for the use of the Committee on Foreign Affairs

Available via the World Wide Web: http://www.foreignaffairs.house.gov/ or http://www.gpo.gov/fdsys/

U.S. GOVERNMENT PRINTING OFFICE

88–730PDF   WASHINGTON : 2014

For sale by the Superintendent of Documents, U.S. Government Printing Office
Internet: bookstore.gpo.gov   Phone: toll free (866) 512–1800; DC area (202) 512–1800
Fax: (202) 512–2104   Mail: Stop IDCC, Washington, DC 20402–0001

COMMITTEE ON FOREIGN AFFAIRS

EDWARD R. ROYCE, California, *Chairman*

CHRISTOPHER H. SMITH, New Jersey
ILEANA ROS-LEHTINEN, Florida
DANA ROHRABACHER, California
STEVE CHABOT, Ohio
JOE WILSON, South Carolina
MICHAEL T. McCAUL, Texas
TED POE, Texas
MATT SALMON, Arizona
TOM MARINO, Pennsylvania
JEFF DUNCAN, South Carolina
ADAM KINZINGER, Illinois
MO BROOKS, Alabama
TOM COTTON, Arkansas
PAUL COOK, California
GEORGE HOLDING, North Carolina
RANDY K. WEBER SR., Texas
SCOTT PERRY, Pennsylvania
STEVE STOCKMAN, Texas
RON DeSANTIS, Florida
DOUG COLLINS, Georgia
MARK MEADOWS, North Carolina
TED S. YOHO, Florida
SEAN DUFFY, Wisconsin
CURT CLAWSON, Florida

ELIOT L. ENGEL, New York
ENI F.H. FALEOMAVAEGA, American
  Samoa
BRAD SHERMAN, California
GREGORY W. MEEKS, New York
ALBIO SIRES, New Jersey
GERALD E. CONNOLLY, Virginia
THEODORE E. DEUTCH, Florida
BRIAN HIGGINS, New York
KAREN BASS, California
WILLIAM KEATING, Massachusetts
DAVID CICILLINE, Rhode Island
ALAN GRAYSON, Florida
JUAN VARGAS, California
BRADLEY S. SCHNEIDER, Illinois
JOSEPH P. KENNEDY III, Massachusetts
AMI BERA, California
ALAN S. LOWENTHAL, California
GRACE MENG, New York
LOIS FRANKEL, Florida
TULSI GABBARD, Hawaii
JOAQUIN CASTRO, Texas

AMY PORTER, *Chief of Staff*   THOMAS SHEEHY, *Staff Director*
JASON STEINBAUM, *Democratic Staff Director*

(III)

CONTENTS

THE RISE OF ISIL: IRAQ AND BEYOND

TUESDAY, JULY 15, 2014

House of Representatives,
Subcommittee on Terrorism, Nonproliferation, and Trade
and
Subcommittee on the Middle East and North Africa,
Committee on Foreign Affairs,
Committee on Foreign Affairs,
Washington, DC.

The subcommittees met, pursuant to notice, at 2 o'clock p.m., in room 2172 Rayburn House Office Building, Hon. Ted Poe (chairman of the subcommittee) presiding.

Mr. POE. The subcommittee will come to order.

Without objection, all members may have 5 days to submit statements, questions, extraneous materials for the record, subject to the length limitation in the rules.

The rise of ISIL and its rapid expansion across Syria and Iraq is a great threat to the security of the Middle East, even to the U.S. Just focusing on Iraq, it is not a pleasant picture. Iraq is one of the world's top oil exporters, to the tune of 2.7 million barrels a day. If ISIL continues to march across Iraq, we could see most of Iraq's exports dry up.

The result would be a spike in oil prices. More countries would want to buy oil, then, from Iran, threatening our sanctions regime. The U.S. economy would also be affected and Americans could lose their jobs.

As Iraqi Prime Minister Maliki looks to a supreme leader in Iran for help, Iranian influence in Iraq is growing day by day. This is disturbing. Also, to me, corruption seems to be a problem in the Maliki regime.

Iranians are bringing in planeloads of weapons and even conducting air strikes. Increased Iranian involvement plays into the worst fears of Iraq's Sunni neighbors like Saudi Arabia. The fear is that the crisis could turn into a regional sectarian war. If this happens, the oil market could spike like never before. Plus, our ally, Israel, would be caught in the middle of a Middle East war.

ISIL may be regionally focused for now, but it has said it has sights on the United States. Today ISIL controls more territory than core al-Qaeda did before 9/11. Planning attacks on the United States costs money, but ISIL has millions of dollars in the bank and seems to be getting more every day.

An attack also takes fighters, and ISIL has thousands of highly trained fighters who are much more capable than those who were fighting in Iraq in 2007 and 2008. Some of these fighters have European passports. This means they can travel to the United States without a visa. Planning attacks takes willingness, and in July 2012 al-Baghdadi warned the U.S. leaders that ''The war with you has just begun.'' In January 2014 he said again about the United States, ''Soon you will be in direct conflict, God permitting, against your will.''

This didn't have to happen. The rise of ISIL was not a surprise. It was just ignored by many in the U.S. It seems to me the White House did not push Maliki hard enough to make the kind of reforms necessary to prevent the crisis in his own government or the army. Mosul fell in 3 hours because Maliki had spent the last 5 years purging the army of all of its effective commanders. And when the Iraqi army came into conflict with ISIL, many soldiers cut and ran, dropping U.S. equipment into the hands of ISIL. Isn't that lovely?

So Maliki has continued to turn Iraq into his own personal fiefdom. Within hours of the withdrawal of U.S. forces in December 2011, Maliki sought the arrest of Vice President and a longtime Sunni rival and sentenced him to death in abstentia. Three years later, Maliki has not learned his lesson.

Just last week he fired his Kurdish Foreign Minister, accused Kurdistan of harboring ISIL terrorists, even though it is the Kurds who have been the best fighters against ISIL. In fact, the last time I was in Iraq with other Members of Congress we asked Maliki some tough questions. And when we got through meeting with him, he ordered us out of his country. He evicted us, in other words.

However, we did stick around and visited with the Kurds, who are very receptive to the United States and support the United States. The Kurds are tired of Maliki's bullying. The Kurds have been long-time friends of the U.S., and if they want independence my opinion is we should support that.

The question is: What does the United States do with Maliki, his incompetence in the rise of ISIL? Like 2010, we are now at another crucial juncture. Maliki and his State of Law Coalition are in the process of trying to form a new government. He is trying to run for a third term. In my opinion, he needs to go. And like what we did in 2010, the U.S. must work with our friends and allies in the region to encourage new leadership.

In the next week, hundreds of American military advisors currently in Iraq are expected to report their findings of Iraq military capability and the strength of ISIL. Congress should be able to see this finished assessment, and I hope my colleagues will join me in this request.

The crisis in ISIL is not really a surprise, but now that it is a reality, what is the U.S. plan to address this aggression?

I will now turn to my ranking member, Mr. Brad Sherman from California, for his 5-minute opening statement.

Mr. SHERMAN. We have seen a Mr. Baghdadi with incredible ego declare himself caliph. We have seen attacks on Mosul, where the Iraqi army was so panicked they didn't even take the money out of the vaults for themselves, their government, or even burn it. We see battles in Tikrit now as that Iraqi army shows a little sign of strength.

In Syria, we have the reasonable Sunni elements comprising by far the least powerful of the three elements fighting for that country, although I guess you could say that the IS, formerly ISIS or ISIL, is not fighting for the country of Syria but for a worldwide caliphate that just happens to include Syria.

The Maliki and the politicians of Baghdad are less than inspiring, but they have just in the last 24 hours agreed on a Sunni to serve as speaker, who achieved that with Shi'ite and Kurdish support, meaning it is the first tripartisan decision or tri-ethnic/religious decision made in Baghdad in recent memory.

The Iraqi goverment—military is not just incapable, but as The New York Times cited yesterday, it is so deeply infiltrated, either with Sunni extremists in some units or Shi'ite personnel backed by Iran in others, that to assign an American advisor is to put that American advisor at risk from the people they are supposedly advising.

Iran, I think, continues to be the greatest threat to us in the Middle East. There is the economics of 2.7 million barrels a day of oil exported chiefly from the Shi'ite areas of southern Iraq. That is 7 percent of global exports, but well less than that in terms of total world production. And I don't think that that oil is likely to be disrupted, because I don't think that the new caliph, as he styles himself, is going to be able to get that far south.

We are faced with a Middle East based on really three divisions. We have got the Sunni extremists, al-Qaeda and the Islamic State, with Hamas, aided to some degree by Qatar, which sometimes pretends to be our ally and friend. We have got a Shi'ite alliance headed by Iran, Assad, Hezbollah, and elements of the Iraqi Government. Perhaps you would classify Maliki as fitting into that group.

And, finally, you have the moderate Shi'ites, including the weakest elements of Syria, that many on this committee thought we should have been supporting long ago. Now it is hard to find credible Sunni moderates to support in the region. Also, including in this group Saudi Araba, the Emirates, Jordan, perhaps Turkey, and the Kurdish non-sovereigns, non-state.

The Sunni extremists pose the greatest threat of a moderate attack against the United States. They have been trying to in effect down one of our planes ever since 9/11. But it is the Shi'ite alliance headed by Iran that poses the threat of a great history-altering catastrophe.

And so as we focus on Baghdad, we shouldn't just say, "Well, Maliki deserves our help because we were stupid enough to install him in that position," nor can we say, "Well, Maliki would be behaving better if only the American President had a different personality." We must recognize that Maliki is part of an Iranian-led alliance, first and foremost, though perhaps the element in that alliance more subject to reason that the others.

So I look forward to hearing from our witnesses about a Middle East that has become more complex every year I serve on this committee. And I yield back.

Mr. POE. I want to recognize the chairman of the Subcommittee on the Middle East and North Africa. I want you to know, first of all, that all of these people here today are here to wish you a happy birthday.

Ms. Ros-Lehtinen. Thirty-nine and holding, Mr. Chairman. That is my story——

Mr. Poe. So congratulations on your birthday.

Ms. Ros-Lehtinen [continuing]. And I am sticking to it.

Mr. Poe. And now you may give your opening statement.

Ms. Ros-Lehtinen. Well, thank you so much, Judge Poe. I would like to recognize, first of all, the several Iraqi veterans that we have serving on our committee. We thank you for your service and for your efforts in fighting the extremists and terrorists in Iraq.

The chaos that the Islamic State of Iraq and the Levant, ISIL, is creating in the region must concern us all. I would point out that though the administration seems to have been surprised by the resurgence of al-Qaeda in Iraq through ISIL, our two subcommittees have been following this issue closely for quite some time, and have been raising the warning flags that can no longer be ignored.

So it isn't as if this was a new problem that came out of nowhere. In our hearing in November, we had Deputy Assistant Secretary for Iraq and Iran, Brett McGurk, testifying and he said that the Iraqis didn't even believe that they, in cooperation with the Sunni coalition groups, the Sons of Iraq, could fend off ISIL, and he said, "They don't think they are going to win because the al-Qaeda groups have better weapons and better resources."

And we know what happened in Mosul and other cities in Iraq. And because they had nowhere else to run, many of the Sons of Iraq turned to join their foes and became members of ISIL. This Iraq crisis has been exacerbated by our failure to act early on in Syria, and also our inability to confront Iran's influence over Iraqi Prime Minister Maliki.

Maliki's marginalization of Iraq's Sunni groups and other non-Shi'a Iraqis is a large reason why Iraq is seeing so much sectarian violence. And for the sake of Iraq and regional security, Maliki must either find a way to make the government more inclusive of all parties or he must step aside. Yet now the administration has said on numerous occasions that it is considering cooperation with Iran and Syria in Iraq to fight ISIL, the very same Iran that has been supporting Assad in Syria, fueling the conflict there, giving ISIL terrorists safe haven to spread their fight in Iraq.

And this is the same Iran that is the world's foremost state sponsor of terrorism that actively, even while the administration negotiates on Iran's nuclear program, targets U.S. national security interests and those of our allies like the democratic Jewish state of Israel. Under no circumstances should the administration seek cooperation with Iran over Iraq or anywhere else. To do so would be folly, and it would be against everything that we in the United States stand for.

The instability that ISIL has created threatens the entire region, but, more importantly, it is also a very real step, a real danger at the doorstep of our ally, the Kingdom of Jordan. Just 2 weeks ago, Congressman Ted Deutch and I went to Jordan to discuss ISIL, the Syrian conflict, other regional issues. And when speaking with the King of Jordan, he was unambiguous when he told us that ISIL poses a grave risk, not just because of the violence but because of the form of radical Islam that it is spreading.

The administration must formalize a decisive policy that outlines our strategic goals and objectives that can help Jordan and other nations counter this militant Islamic threat. We need actions from this administration. We needed them months ago. ISIL is only getting more threatening and large while the administration is still pondering its policy.

It has large financial assets that help keep it afloat, much of which is gained from seizing cash from banks and selling oil in the black market. And last week it claimed to have seized nuclear materials. These terrorists must be stopped or else we risk serious implications for our future security.

Thank you, Mr. Chairman, for this hearing.

Mr. POE. I will now turn to the ranking member of the Subcommittee on the Middle East and North Africa, Mr. Ted Deutch from Florida, for his 5-minute opening statement.

Mr. DEUTCH. I thank you, Mr. Chairman, and Mr. Ranking Member, and to my chairman, birthday greetings to you as well.

When violence in Syria broke out nearly 3½ years ago, we were troubled by the reports of how rapidly extremist forces seemed to be taking hold. Groups like Jabhat al-Nusra and other loosely affiliated al-Qaeda groups employed grisly tactics and seemed bent on turning Syria into a terrorist safe haven. Fast forward, however, to this past February when al-Qaeda leadership disavowed a group that it deemed too extreme, the Islamic State of Iraq and Syria, now commonly known as ISIS or ISIL.

ISIL, which formed out of al-Qaeda in Iraq, has recently renamed itself the Islamic State and has been expanding its stronghold in Syria before returning to Iraq. With the world still focused on the Syrian conflict, ISIS domination in Iraq may have seemed to come out of nowhere, but the political and security conditions on the ground in Iraq have been breeding an environment ripe for jihadist takeover.

Since the last United States soldier left Iraq, the situation has been rapidly deteriorating. In February, the full Foreign Affairs Committee held a hearing on al-Qaeda in Iraq, where we assessed that violence this past year in Iraq had reached levels not seen since 2006. The Iraqi security forces, which the U.S. spent billions of dollars training and equipping, preferred to abandon their posts rather than fight a brutal militant group.

Prime Minister Maliki's inability over 8 years to nurture an inclusive political system has marginalized Sunnis in Baghdad and tribal leaders throughout the country. Unlike in years past where Sunni tribal leaders united to help fight extremist threats, Maliki's attempts to consolidate power created space between his government and Sunni constituencies just wide enough for ISIL to fill. In fact, just days ago, The Washington Post ran a story entitled, ''In Baghdad Middle Class Sunnis Say They Prefer Militants to Maliki.''

Who can play mediator with the Sunni leaders to convince that it is within their interest to disassociate from and disavow ISIL? Certainly, we are not going to fight for a Maliki government that refuses to engage in any political reconciliation.

Conflict in the region has given way to a myriad of strange bedfellows. Let me be clear: We are not in partnership with Iran and

Iraq. And as Mr. Eisenstadt has pointed out, continued suggestions to the contrary will only threaten U.S. interests. It is clear that the Iranians have an interest in saving Maliki, and they have a long history of training and arming Shi'ite militias.

With many of the resources committed to keeping Assad afloat, and sustaining his violence front with Syria, how involved are the Iranians prepared to get? Will they shift Hezbollah fighters to Iraq or encourage their other terrorist beneficiaries to join the fight? And with ISIL's newly found financial independence, is there any foreign actor that can influence the organization?

More powerfully, the question for the panel is: Can ISIL be stopped? Many are already talking as if a breakup states and rejittering of borders is inevitable. The most recent scenario emerging from many experts for Iraq appears to be some sort of loose confederation of Kurdistan, a Shi'ite area, and a Sunni area under a weak central government. What would that mean for the region? What effect would this have on U.S. interests?

As Chairman Ros-Lehtinen pointed out, we were recently in Jordan where much attention has been focused on the ISIL threat. ''Is Jordan the next target?'' I ask our panel. Can Jordanian forces hold its border with Iraq? The United States and our reigonal partners have to do everything we can to support Jordan. The Kingdom has been a stable voice of moderation and has kept its borders open to those seeking refuge from the Syrian crisis, despite its already strained economy and resources.

It remains to be seen how far ISIL's reach will extend, as it appears momentum has slowed the closer fighting gets to Baghdad, a Shi'ite stronghold. Shi'ite militias and the Iraqi army appear to be bent on preventing Baghdad from falling, though this does not preclude the possibility of a series of deadly attacks by ISIL as they attempt to weaken Baghdad.

So far President Obama has responded to this very real threat by deploying Marines for Embassy security. With 1,700 personnel still on the ground, the United States must remain extremely vigilant if the security situation around Baghdad deteriorates. There are fears that an attack or attempted attack on the Embassy or U.S. persons might drive the United States into the conflict.

While we can continue to provide some support to various Iraqi elements in this fight, the United States should not inject itself into this sectarian war. We lost too many brave American soldiers to a misguided war in Iraq, and the American people deserve a thoughtful U.S. response with serious consideration of our national security interests, both at home and in the region.

I remain deeply concerned that ISIL's pronouncement of a new caliphate could attract hundreds or thousands of new fighters coming to train with this group of terrorists. What happens when they return home to North Africa or Europe or elsewhere?

I would like to thank our very distinguished panel for being here, and I look forward to the discussion.

Mr. POE. I thank the gentleman. Just so everyone knows, we are in the midst of votes. It is the hope of the Chair that we get through the opening statements and then we will have testimony. At 3 o'clock we will start testimony.

The Chair recognizes the gentleman from Ohio, Mr. Chabot, for 1 minute.

Mr. CHABOT. Thank you, Mr. Chairman. I want to thank Chairman Ros-Lehtinen also for holding this hearing, along with yourself. The Islamic State of Iraq and the Levant has become one of the greatest threats to the Middle Eastern region.

As ISIL continues to gain control over more territory throughout Syria and Iraq, U.S. strategic interests will inevitably be at even greater risk. There are reports that ISIL now maintains training camps in Iraq and Syria. And although they may not yet have the capability to carry out operations here in the United States, that may change as the group continues to recruit Western passport holders with the intent of returning them back to their home countries, including the United States, to commit acts of terrorism.

The U.S. lost thousands of American lives and spent well over $1 trillion in Iraq. It is extremely disheartening to see a hard-won victory quickly slipping away for short-term political gain, rather than strengthening U.S. long-term strategic interests.

I want to thank you again for calling this hearing, and I yield back.

Mr. POE. The gentleman yields back his time. The Chair recognizes the gentleman from New York, Mr. Higgins.

Mr. HIGGINS. Thank you, Mr. Chairman. First, let us just establish that this is not about freedom and democracy, and it never was. It was always about control and manipulation. And what we have going on in Iraq is really not isolated to Iraq; it is the entire region.

And this dates back to, you know, who the rightful successor to the Prophet Muhammad is. When you look at, you know, an extreme group, the Islamic State of Iraq and Syria, and the leader of that group, Abu Bakr al-Baghdadi, you know, he takes his name from the historic successor to the Prophet Muhammad as viewed by Sunnis. And, you know, Nouri al-Maliki, as a Shi'a, failed to recognize and embrace the Sunni, you know, community, to be part of that society. So, obviously, they have risen up in opposition to this.

So unless and until there is a recognition of pluralism, of minority rights, not only in Iraq and Syria, but throughout the Middle East, you will never have peace there. So I look forward to the testimony by our expert witnesses, and I yield back.

Mr. POE. Thank the gentleman for his comments. The Chair recognizes the gentleman from Illinois, Mr. Kinzinger, for 1 minute.

Mr. KINZINGER. Thank you, Mr. Chairman. And to the great panel, thank you all for being here. It is good to have you.

As a veteran of Iraq, and somebody that was there during the surge, it is extremely disheartening for me to see this absolutely predictable scenario unfolding in front of our eyes. It is sad, and it is, frankly, the worst-case scenario. So we talk about, do we need to preserve the Iraqi standard, or do we let this fight out until there is a political solution in Iraq?

Let me just say that what is happening right now is the worst-case scenario. So any option we have—and I have advocated for pushing ISIS back both in Iraq and in Syria with air strikes—is a better option than what we are seeing unfold before us.

We are going to hear a lot, I am sure—hear from both Members of Congress and maybe some panelists about the idea of war fatigue. And while it is very real and very understandable, I would just like to remind everybody that thankfully President Truman, at the end of World War II, didn't come back and say, ''We are fatigued of war,'' and bring all the troops home from Europe, or we would see a Soviet Union twice the size as today.

And with that, Mr. Chairman, I yield back.

Mr. POE. I thank the gentleman. The Chair recognizes the gentleman from Rhode Island, Mr. Cicilline, for 1 minute.

Mr. CICILLINE. Thank you, Chairman, and thank you to the ranking members for holding this important joint hearing today on this very critical issue.

The threat that ISIL poses to our national stability is of paramount concern to the United States and our allies, and addressing that threat and working toward a political solution to the instability in Iraq must remain a top priority of U.S. foreign policy. And as we continue to monitor ISIL's insurgency and expansion in Iraq and Syria, we must remain aware of the destabilizing effects of the so-called Islamic State on the entire region, as my colleague from New York just mentioned.

We have to be determined to better understand the violence that currently permeates the Middle East and how the United States can predict, identify, and prevent insurgency and terrorism, and ultimately support peaceful democracy in the region. We must make sure that going forward we promote stability and unity in the region.

I look forward to hearing these very distinguished witnesses today, and thank you for being here, and I yield back.

Mr. POE. The Chair recognizes the gentleman from Pennsylvania, Mr. Perry, for 1 minute.

Mr. PERRY. Thank you, Mr. Chairman. I want to begin by saying that I reject categorically the comments from my colleague, Mr. Higgins. With that, the crisis created by the Islamic State or ISIS or ISIL, or whatever it is called, continues unabated in Iraq, is now on the precipice of full-blown civil war.

As U.S. forces withdrew in 2011, however, President Obama's administration failed to negotiate an agreement with Iraq that would have allowed a limited U.S. presence to help the Iraqis keep al-Qaeda and its affiliates from filling the power vacuum created by withdrawal. Instead, America quickly abandoned Iraq, and in the process allowed ISIS to hold transnational territory from which it has launched terrorist operations.

Both Congress and the Pentagon warned the White House about the worsening situation in Iraq, to no avail. In January, President Obama referred to ISIS as the ''JV team.'' I do wonder if he would like to play the JV team.

This type of what seems to be willful misinformed assessment of our enemy is just another instance of the administration's out-of-touch Iraq, Russia, Iran, Syria, you-name-it policy.

With that, I yield back.

Mr. POE. The gentleman yields back. The Chair recognizes the gentleman from Illinois, Mr. Schneider, for 1 minute.

Mr. SCHNEIDER. Thank you, Mr. Chairman. It is clear that we are living through an inflection point in history. In particular, the current situation in Iraq lies at the confluence of four seams of conflict. The first two sources of conflict date back more than a millennium, and they reflect the divide between Sunnis and Shi'a on the one hand and between Persians and Arabs on the other.

The third source of conflict arises from the collapse of the artificial nation states created a century ago by the Sykes-Picot agreement, in particular now in Syria and Iraq where we see them declining. Finally, in recent decades, we have seen the emergence of radical Islam merge with the threat of global jihad and international terrorism.

In the chaos of Syria and Iraq, forces of global jihad and international terrorism such as al-Qaeda, al-Nusra, and now ISIS, have found fertile breeding ground for the culture of death and destruction. It is clear, whether we like it or not, that the United States must remain engaged in the region to deny radical Islamic militants a training ground to target our allies in the region and the U.S. homeland.

I look forward to hearing from our witnesses on how we can achieve our national security goals in Iraq while working to address the long-term root causes of unrest in the region.

And with that, I yield back.

Mr. POE. The gentleman yields back. The Chair recognizes the gentleman from Virginia, Mr. Connolly, for 1 minute.

Mr. CONNOLLY. I thank the chair. And I wish Mr. Perry was still here, because I disagree with him. You know, we have the distinguished General Jack Keane as one of our witnesses today, and he wrote an op-ed in which he uses the phrase ''setting aside for the moment the question of whether the administration has the will to intervene again in Iraq.''

With all due respect, I don't think that is the question at all, nor is it one to be set-aside. The American people do not want this intervention. You know, 63 percent to 29 percent oppose sending U.S. ground troops back into Iraq. When asked about air strikes, a plurality of 39 percent would prefer the U.S. not conduct air stikes.

This is the second-longest war in our history, and it does limit our options. And I might add, no matter what some of my friends on the other side of the aisle want to say, ISIS is not the creation of this administration, nor is the unsettlement in Iraq the responsibility of this administration. To say otherwise is to ignore history.

Thank you, Mr. Chairman.

Mr. POE. The gentleman yields back.

The subcommittee will be in recess until 3 o'clock. We will reconvene at that time, 3 o'clock.

[Recess.]

Mr. POE. This subcommittees will come to order.

Without objection, all of the witnesses' prepared statements will be made part of the record. I ask that each witness please keep your presentation to no more than 5 minutes. I will introduce the witnesses and then give time for opening statements.

The Honorable James Jeffrey is the Philip Solondz Distiniguished Visiting Fellow at The Washington Institute for

Near East Policy. Ambassador Jeffrey previously served in the United States Army and was Ambassador to Iraq from 2010 to 2012.

General Jack Keane is the chairman of the board at the Institute for the Study of War. General Keane is a retired four-star General and the former Vice Chief of Staff for the United States Army.

Mr. Doug Bandow is a senior fellow at the Cato Institute where he specializes in foreign policy and civil liberties. Previously, Mr. Bandow was a visiting fellow at the Heritage Foundation and served as Special Assistant to President Ronald Reagan.

And Mr. Michael Eisenstadt is a senior fellow and the director of the Military and Security Studies Program at The Washington Institute for Near East Policy. Mr. Eisenstadt has been on active duty in Iraq twice as part of his service in the United States Army Reserve, once in 2008 and then again in 2010.

First of all, thank you, gentlemen, for your service. And, Ambassador Jeffrey, we will start with you. And you have 5 minutes.

STATEMENT OF THE HONORABLE JAMES JEFFREY, PHILIP SOLONDZ DISTINGUISHED VISITING FELLOW, THE WASHINGTON INSTITUTE FOR NEAR EAST POLICY (FORMER U.S. AMBASSADOR TO IRAQ)

Ambassador JEFFREY. Thank you very much. Chairman Poe, Ranking Member Sherman, Chairman Ros-Lehtinen, it is an honor to be here today on such an important issue.

As we heard from the statements from members of the two subcommittees, the turn of events in Iraq over the last month leading to the establishment of the so-called Islamic State is a stunning blow to U.S. policy and goals in the Middle East. The creation of an extremist quasi-state analogous to Afghanistan under the Taliban exposes many of our key interests globally as well as in the region. Simultaneously, we are facing a militant Iran on the march, allied with Syria's Assad, Hezbollah, and some in Iraq.

This is an emergency, not an everyday crisis. At this point—and this has already been suggested—the cost of doing nothing significant now is greater than the risks of most actions short of actually committing ground troops.

The question was asked a bit earlier, can ISIS be stopped? I think it can. The policy laid down by President Obama on June 19, which is focused on mobilizing intelligence, military resources, while trying to get an inclusive government based on the idea that we need an inclusive government for any retaking of these areas that ISIS has seized, primarily in the Sunni Arab areas of Iraq, in principle is a good way forward.

The problem is, this policy was announced almost a month ago. We have seen almost nothing happen on the ground since then, other than some of the assets have been moved forward and an assessment has been done. The only good piece of news that has come out of this so far is just today that the Iraqi Parliament has elected, by a significant majority, a speaker, Salim al-Jabari. I know him. He is a good choice. He is from the Sunni Arab population. But the Parliament then fell into rangling over which Shi'a deputy would be selected, suggesting that the whole issue of Mr. Maliki has not been decided yet.

To achieve our goals, to carry out the policy that the President laid out, several things must happen very quickly. First of all, we do need a new government, and this government cannot include Prime Minister Maliki at the helm. He has lost all credibility with the Kurds and with the Sunni Arab population, and his own performance as Commander-in-Chief is one of the reasons why the military did so badly.

For many reasons, Iraq needs a new Prime Minister. That is the most important thing for turning this situation around, but it has to be done quickly. The Kurds must be brought back into the Iraqi camp. They are toying with the idea of independence right now. There are offerings that can be made to them, particularly in the banking and oil areas, that would entice back I think, assuming Maliki goes, but that has to be done quickly.

The Sunni Arab regions and the specific provinces have to be offered the kind of deal that some of the oil provinces—I am thinking of Basra, Kirkuk, the Kurdish region, and Najaf, which receives a lot of tourists—have gotten from the central government. Thye have been able to share in the central government's oil wells, and they have been able to develop their own economies and have some control over local governance. This is a good model that could be applied very quickly.

Finally, we need a Commander-in-Chief of the Iraqi forces that is not the Prime Minister. That position has to be split. With those three concrete actions, we could bring back most of the people, most of the political forces, behind a new government and a new Prime Minister and a new President very quickly.

At the same time, the U.S. should begin conducting limited strikes as this process goes on to deter ISIS from pushing forward and providing support not just for the Iraqi army and Maliki's forces but for Sunni tribes and others who are fighting on the Euphrates Valley and to the Kurds as well. We do need to limit these strikes until such time as we can get an inclusive government, because the retaking of these Sunni areas will be a very long-term operation.

Finally, we need to provide support to the Syrian rebels, a $500,000 program that the President has proposed. Failing this, we will very quickly, as also was mentioned earlier, be facing three separate states all posing problems to us—the Iraqi, the Islamic State, a threat to the entire world including the homeland; a rump Shi'a state in the south controlling Iraq's oil wealth and dominated by Iran; and a Kurdistan, whose role in the region will be very, very complicated. We need to avoid this if at all possible. We should move forward.

Finally, we should not be coordinating beyond the bare minimum with Iran. They may share some goals with us, but they do not share our interests.

Thank you very much.

[The prepared statement of Ambassador Jeffrey follows:]

TESTIMONY BEFORE THE HOUSE FOREIGN AFFAIRS COMMITTEE

IRAQ

JAMES FRANKLIN JEFFREY, PHILIP SOLONDZ DISTINQUISHED VISITING FELLOW, THE WASHINGTON INSTITUTE FOR NEAR EASTERN POLICY

The turn of events in Iraq over the past month, leading to the establishment of the Islamic State (IS) by the Al Qaeda in Iraq offshoot group Islamic State of Iraq and Levant (ISIL), is a stunning blow to US policy and objectives in the Middle East. The creation of an extremist quasi-state, analogous to Afghanistan under the Taliban, carries the risk of further escalation including a regional Sunni-Shia conflagration, and a dramatic loss in US influence in the region. Simultaneously, in part as trigger, in part as reaction to this development, we are facing a militant Iran on the march, allied with Syria's Assad, Hezbollah, and some in Iraq. The US government must counter both the IS threat and the overall deterioration of stability throughout the region. This is an emergency, not an everyday crisis, and the caution which characterizes US actions often is inappropriate. The costs of doing nothing significant now are greater than the risks of most actions short of committing ground troops.

The significance of this situation can be seen by juxtaposing it with President Obama's description of America's vital interests in the Middle East in his September, 2013 UN General Assembly Speech: responding to external aggression against our allies and partners, ensuring the free flow of energy from the region, dismantling terrorist networks that threaten our people and not tolerating the development or use of weapons of mass destruction. The rise of the IS, with control over up to six million people and massive military equipment and funding, in close proximity to some of the largest oil fields in the world, and bordering our NATO ally Turkey and security partners Jordan, Saudi Arabia, and Kuwait, threatens three of the President's four vital interests. The situation if it deteriorates further will likely threaten the fourth, development of weapons of mass destruction, as Iran is even less likely to forego such weapons in the face of a possible regional conflict arising from the IS threat.

The President's course of action outlined in his Iraq speech of June 19th is sensible: protect our Baghdad embassy, strengthen our intelligence and military presence in and around Iraq, increase assistance to the Iraqi military, and press the Iraqi political system to support a new, inclusive government which can reach out to estranged Sunni Arabs and Kurds and maintain the country's unity; only then with our help can it begin to retake areas held by the IS. Consider this Plan A. While this remains the best option, and actions to achieve it are discussed below, it is not clear if we still have time to achieve it. Iraq is functionally split into three states—the IS, the Kurdistan Regional Government (KRG), and rump Iraq governed out of Baghdad, which is almost entirely cut off from the KRG by the IS and marauding Sunni insurgents. Mass murders of Sunni and Shia prisoners and civilians by Shia militias and ISIL respectively exacerbate the divisions further. The Administration thus must focus on a Plan B in case Iraq's current divisions grow even deeper.

PLAN A

To achieve the President's objective of a unified, inclusive Iraq to which we can provide significant new military assistance including air strikes, the following needs to occur in the days ahead:

--The Iraqi parliament, charged with forming a new government after the March elections, must decide on a prime minister other than Nuri al Maliki. There is absolutely no chance of Iraq remaining united, or of the Iraqi security forces performing effectively, or of an inclusive government appealing to Kurds and Sunni Arabs, with him still at the helm. The ink in written commitments by Iraqi leaders to reach out to other communities over the past 11 years would fill several bathtubs; what is needed is not new promises, but concrete action. The most convincing such action would be for Maliki to step down, failing that, for the Shia parties to coalesce behind essentially any alternative candidate to force him out. Maliki is rightly associated with the worse forms of sectarianism, and only his departure would convince now highly skeptical Kurds and Sunni Arabs that a Shia Arab-dominated political system will take their concerns into account. Removing Maliki is a job for the Iraqis, not the US, and Washington has to be careful not to advocate his departure openly, as that will only strengthen him. But we must make clear that serious US military engagement, now desperately needed, will come only with a different leadership.

--The Kurds must be brought back into the Iraqi camp. Their dispute with Maliki and on a larger level Baghdad has grown more serious since Mosul fell, due to serious errors by both Erbil and Baghdad. Finding a replacement for Maliki is necessary but not sufficient to win the Kurds back. This will require further compromises on Kurdish oil exports and building on a December 2013 agreement not carried out, and Baghdad needs to restart payment of the Kurds' 17% share of southern oil exports. In turn the Kurds, as they have acknowledged, will have to share their oil proceeds 17-83% between themselves and Baghdad, and exercise restraint on the status of the Kirkuk field now in their military power. The US, once the above measures are taken, should pressure both the Kurds and their not-so-silent patron, Turkey, to participate fully in the central government, and cease threatening an independence referendum. What's in this for the Kurds? Full independence is a chimera given not only Iranian but Turkish sensitivities, a 17% share of all Iraq's oil exports will earn Erbil more money than exporting from the north, even with Kirkuk, for the next few years at least, and tranquility between Erbil and Baghdad will allow both to focus on the greater threat—IS.

--The new Iraqi leadership should make clear that it will institute similar oil earnings distribution policies to the Sunni provinces, along the lines seen to some degree with the KRG and oil producing provinces. While politicians' promises to distribute wealth equitably and promote economic development are fine, they have been heard many times with little results, especially in Sunni areas. Only such a dramatic, concrete commitment will win credibility in the Sunni areas.

--The U.S. should begin very limited strikes against ISIL elements to support Kurdish Peshmerga, Sunni Arab tribal fighters, and Iraqi central government security forces when the latter are defending the approaches to Baghdad or other majority Shia population areas. Such strikes could shift the military momentum away from IS, and show all those fighting it that the US, under the right conditions, not only will strike IS, but will strike it much harder. Given prior Administration reluctance to use military force, such demonstrations now are necessary. Limited US strikes could leverage our efforts for an inclusive central government. But we would have to be careful, as the President said, not to give the impression that we are taking sides with a sectarian government against the Sunnis. The strikes thus would have to be coordinated with friendly Iraqi Sunni Arabs and regional partners.

--Simultaneously, the US should rapidly deploy its $500 million committed to train and equip the Syrian opposition. The US should begin strikes against IS in Syria, and once significant US-trained and equipped forces are in the field, strike against Syrian government forces opposing them.

--Once these steps have been taken, the U.S. can plan with the Iraqi government, KRG, friendly Iraqi Sunni Arabs, and regional partners, to retake those Iraqi areas now held by the IS. Such a counter-insurgency plan would include aggressive US training, equipping, and coordinating, intelligence, and air strikes, along with action by Sunni Arabs willing with our help to take on IS.

PLAN B

While the above offers the best way forward, it may soon be too late to implement it, as the divisions between the various Iraqi groups deepen, the KRG moves towards virtual independence, and Maliki entrenches himself in office.

Were this to occur, the US must deal with three separate entities, all posing significant problems for American interests: an IS threatening us, as well as our allies and partners, and a magnet for jihadist supporters world-wide; a KRG moving ever more towards a de jure breakup with Baghdad, raising the specter of a Near East-wide quest for a Kurdish nation state, and undermining existing borders; and a rump Iraq, dominated by Shia religious parties heavily influenced by Iran, and controlling what the International Energy Agency believes could well be exports of six million barrels of oil by 2020—almost two thirds of Saudi Arabia's exports.

Under these circumstances, the US should:

----deter and if necessary defeat IS attacks on Jordan and other partners and allies. This is the sine qua non of any effective American role. To carry it out the Administration must concede that its policies have generated huge doubts about America's military reliability. Thus actions, not just words.

--coordinate policies with Turkey, Jordan, Israel, and the Gulf States. That is easy to write but hard to implement. It would have to include more active US support for the Syrian opposition, agreement with other states on whom to support within it, and caution with the KRG, neither endorsing a independent status anathema not just to Baghdad but to Arab states, nor opposing KRG-Turkish cooperation on oil exports and security.

--conduct strikes against IS in both Iraq and Syria.

--recalibrate US policy towards Baghdad; to the extent it is willing to cooperate with us, and avoid provoking the Kurds and the Sunni Arabs further, then limited US military support under the FMS program should continue, as should direct US military action against IS attacks against Shia population centers. This policy will require constant review depending upon how influential Iran becomes in Baghdad, and how relations develop between Baghdad and its Kurdish and Sunni Arab citizens.

IRAN

The US should maintain limited exchanges with Iran on Iraq, as at a superficial level (unity of the state, fight against IS), there are common interests. But there are no common goals, and the Administration must be cautious in giving any impression that there is one. Here the mess that the Middle East has become severely hampers US freedom of action. Essentially, we see not one but two hegemonic Islamic radical forces intent on overthrowing the prevailing nation state order in the region—Al Qaeda especially IS, and the Islamic Republic of Iran. Importantly, our allies in the common struggle for stability—Turkey, Israel, and the Sunni Arab states—see Iran as at least an equal threat to their survival as Al Qaeda, and we must respect that to gain their essential cooperation.

On the other hand, we should not be drawn into a regional "Sunni versus Shia" conflict. Such a conflict would tear the region apart, and any US involvement would have us violating our "we fight for liberal principles, not sectarian interests" policy that we have been able to maintain in the region and elsewhere, such as in the Balkans.

LESSONS FROM THE PAST

Much has been written blaming this or the last Administration, or this or that decision, for the crisis in Iraq and in the region. But the situation is so serious now that any way out of it will require decisive, difficult US action predicated on support from the American people. Thus, the less polemics about the past, the better. But there are certain lessons from our regional involvement since 2001, and earlier, that we should heed:

--As we've experienced, from Al Qaeda before 9/11 to Iraq since 2011, problems in the region absent decisive, heads up engagement by the US will keep getting worse to the point when, very late, and at great cost, the US will be compelled to act at far greater cost and risk than if acting earlier.

--Dramatic efforts to transform the underlying historical, political, social, ethnic-religious and ideological fundamentals of the Middle East are bound to fail. We have to deal with a dysfunctional region as it is.

--Putting American ground troops into Middle Eastern conflicts, as seen from Beirut and Mogadishu to Kabul and Baghdad, is a recipe for disaster unless they have as in 1991 a clear, achievable, purely military limited mission.

--But using limited force, from the air or sea, or through our allies, special operations, or other surrogates, must remain a major element in our response to regional instability, crisis and war. Such limited actions do not incur major costs, have limited escalation risks, and have repeatedly been tolerated or supported by the American people.

--Such measures are much in demand now. The Administration's 'not doing stupid stuff' admonishment is defined so broadly that any use of limited or indirect force is rejected as tantamount to another Iraq level 'adventure.' This thinking has brought us to the brink of disaster.

Mr. POE. Thank you, Ambassador.
General Keane, you have 5 minutes.

STATEMENT OF GENERAL JACK KEANE, USA, RETIRED, CHAIRMAN OF THE BOARD, INSTITUTE FOR THE STUDY OF WAR

General KEANE. Chairman, Ranking Members, and members of the committee, thank you for inviting me. You know, ISIL is the new face of the al-Qaeda and the much larger radical Islamic movement. ISIL has accomplished what the 9/11 al-Qaeda only dreamt about but truly forfeited when they overreached and attacked the American people.

As we know, ISIL in 3 years has managed to take control of a vast swath of territory in Syria and Iraq. They declared an Islamist State, they have got somebody in charge of it—al-Baghdadi—designated him as a caliph. How did all of this happen? And was it a surprise? Absolutely not.

The United States Intelligence Agency had been quite aware of this threat for a time and have been reporting it. This is a failure of policymakers who essentially ignored it. ISIL systematically took control of territory in Syria, preferring this territorial control and imposing its own harsh form of governance to actually fighting the Assad regime.

Two years ago ISIL began a concentrated terrorist campaign in Mosul, Anbar province, and Baghdad. These terrorist activities were a prelude to the army-like conventional attack that ISIL made to seize Fallujah, eventually Mosul, and much of northern Iraq.

ISIL represents the most menacing threat to the Middle East stability that I have observed, with stated objectives to expand to Jordan and beyond. Obviously, ISIL is a threat to U.S. national security objectives in the Middle East, and eventually a threat to the American people as it becomes a vast breeding ground for foreign fighters, to include Americans, some of which has already occurred as reported by Mr. Clapper, the Director of National Intelligence. In my view, this will only get worse.

ISIL must be stopped. It should be our top priority. And it only will be accomplished with the United States in the lead, with cooperation with our allies in the region. This is not an impenetrable force. It is relatively small, under 10,000, and because of their harsh rule they are very unpopular. ISIL's rapid success is due to its army-like conventional tactics, which is also its major vulnerability.

ISIL can be effectively attacked in Syria and Iraq using airpower to destroy known sanctuary staging bases, lines of communication, and command and control facilities. Special operation forces should be clandestinely employed to attack high value targets, particularly in Iraq but eventually expanded into Syria.

The President's decision to assist the Free Syrian Army is a step in the right direction. Before the recent Iraq invasion, the Free Syrian Army was the only force in Syria that fought ISIL. Iraq needs our help, certainly. There is much we can do to assist Iraq diplomatically, politically, and militarily.

I associate myself with Ambassador Jeffrey's comments. And I would just add that I also think diplomatically Secretary Kerry should lead an effort to work with Sunni leaders in the region—Saudi Arabia, Jordan, Qatar—who have relationships with Iraq Sunni politicians and Sunni tribal leaders, to move them away from ISIL

Politically, disptach to Iraq, a team led by Ambassador Crocker and General David Petraeus, to work with the Iraq political and military leadership to move them toward a unity government who reconciles with the Sunni tribes and brings back the Kurds.

On the military side, the rapid collapse of the Iraq army was a major surprise. Maliki systematically purged military leaders, many who distinguished themselves during the surge in 2007. He replaced them with cronies and hacks who, over time, drove down the morale of the units, and some of those units that fled in the face of the ISIL advance were only at 50 percent strength.

U.S. advisors can assist with the reconstruction of Iraqi army units that disintegrated along with establishing and overseeing a necessary training program. Advisors can also help with the defense of Baghdad, planning it, and also executing it, and also with the planning and execution of a counter-offensive to retake lost territory.

Special forces, air-ground controllers, and airpower can certainly assist in doing all of that. To do nothing more, diplomatically, politically, and militarily, however, almost guarantees with certainty that Iraq, as the world knew it, it will be gone—some believe it is already—with the prospect of ISIL dominating most of the country.

The fact of the matter is that Iran and Russia see this upheaval as an opportunity to advance their national interest in the region, and they are all in. Let me conclude by simply saying that this is a time for less hand wringing and about what—or less hand wringing about how we got here and who is at fault, although I am prepared to talk about it, and more focus on U.S. resolve to lead a determined effort to push back and eventually defeat ISIL, which should be a part of a larger comprehensive strategy to assist our partners in the region to stop the rise of radical Islam.

Iraq needs capable, sophisticated U.S. assistance to reconcile its damaging political differences by moving toward a unity government.

Thank you, and I look forward to your questions.

[The prepared statement of General Keane follows:]

Testimony

House Foreign Affairs Committee

Joint Sub Committees

Terrorism, Nonproliferation and Trade

Middle East and North Africa

By

Gen. John M. Keane, USA (Ret)

on

ISIL: Political Turmoil in Iraq

1400 hours, 15 July 14

Rayburn House Office Building

Full Committee Room 2172

Thank you Chairman Poe, Chairman Ros-Lehtinen, ranking members Sherman and Deutch and members of the committee for inviting me to testify today on ISIL and political turmoil in Iraq. Permit me to acknowledge the distinguished panel of which I am honored to be a member.

ISIS as we at the Institute for the Study of War (ISW) reference it will for the purposes of my testimony be referred to as ISIL to be consistent with your desires.

ISIL is the new face of the Al Qaeda and the larger radical Islamist movement. ISIL has already accomplished what the 9/11 Al Qaeda, only dreamt about, but forfeited, when they over reached and attacked the American people. As we know, ISIL in 3 short years has managed to take control of a vast swath of territory, essentially villages, towns and cities from East of Aleppo in Syria through the Iraq / Syria border, rendering that border non-existent, to Anbar province in Iraq, west of Baghdad, to Mosul north of Baghdad, with fighting outside of Baghdad ongoing within a one hour drive. They have declared this territory "The Islamist State", a bonafide caliphate, with al Baghdadi as the head of state. How did this happen? Was it a surprise? Absolutely not.

U.S. intelligence agencies have been quite aware of this threat, this is the failure of policy makers who ignored it. ISW has been monitoring and reporting on ISIL for almost 3 years as it systematically took control of territory in Syria, preferring this territorial control and imposing its own very harsh form of governance to actually fighting the Assad regime. Indeed rarely was there an occurrence where ISIL attacked Assad regime forces or even more bizarre that regime forces ever attacked ISIL, even when ISIL was within striking distance by regime forces. This unusual reality may be explained by the fact that ISIL was the former organization, Al Qaeda in Iraq (AQI) which the Syrian regime facilitated the movement of foreign fighters from Damascus airport to the Syrian / Iraq border into the hands of AQI. AQI was defeated in Iraq by 2009, an admission they made repeatedly in message traffic, calling off the flow of the foreign fighters.

Two years ago ISIL began a concentrated terrorist campaign in Mosul, Anbar province and in Baghdad. Mosul received particular attention with frequent suicide bombings, attacks on police stations and military outposts and last summer they began an assassination campaign to kill prominent government and military officials. These terrorist activities were a prelude to the army like conventional attack that ISIL made to seize Fallujah, eventually Mosul and much of northern Iraq.

ISIL represents the most menacing threat to Middle East stability that I have ever observed with stated objectives to expand to Jordan and beyond. Obviously, ISIL is a threat to US national security objectives in the Middle East and eventually a threat to the American people as it becomes a vast breeding ground for foreign fighters to include Americans, some of which has already occurred, as reported by Mr. Clapper, the Director of National Intelligence. In my view, this will only get worse.

ISIL must be stopped, it should be our top priority and it will only be done with the US in the lead in cooperation with our allies in the region. The US challenge is that we have never had a comprehensive strategy to stop radical Islam or to defeat it. As such it is on the rise throughout the Middle East and

Africa. We desperately need that strategy now and we must begin with ISIL before it doubles and triples in size. This is not an impenetrable force; it is relatively small, under ten thousand, and because of their harsh rule, they are very unpopular. ISIL's rapid success is due to its army like conventional tactics which is also its major vulnerability. ISIL can be effectively attacked in Syria and Iraq using air power to destroy known sanctuaries, staging bases, lines of communication and command and control facilities. Special operation forces should be clandestinely employed to attack high value targets particularly in Iraq but eventually expanded into Syria. The White House decision to assist the Free Syrian Army (FSA) is a step in the right direction. Before the recent Iraq invasion the FSA was the only force in Syria that fought ISIL.

Iraq needs our help certainly. Key policy decisions in 2009 to disengage from Iraq politically and to no longer help shape Iraq's political future was disastrous. Particularly in light of previous success in other post conflicts; Germany, Italy, Japan, South Korea, the Philippines, and Bosnia Herzegovina. Equally damaging in 2011 was leaving no counter terrorism force to pounce on the AQ if they reemerged or advisors to continue with the unfinished business of growing the capacity of the ISF. These US policy failures along with Maliki's political incompetence and malfeasance in undermining his opponents directly contributed to the alienation of Sunni tribes and the success of ISIL.

There is much we can do to assist Iraq, diplomatically, politically and militarily.

- DIPLOMATIC: Secretary Kerry should lead an effort to work with Sunni leaders in the region (Saudi Arabia, Jordan, Qatar) who have relationships with Iraq's Sunni politicians and Sunni tribal leaders to move them away from ISIL, while their ISIL support may provide them with a shortsighted near term gain, it endangers the entire region and the very survival of Iraq.

- POLITICAL: Dispatch to Iraq a team led by Ryan Crocker and David Petraeus to work with the Iraq political and military leadership to move them toward a unity government who reconciles with the reconcilable Sunni tribes (former Saddam Hussein regime Bathists, so called JRTN, are not reconcilable.) It is a known fact that the US envoy team currently in Iraq are only communication facilitators and are not influential in changing behavior.

- MILITARY: General Petraeus who has critical Iraq relationships and can tangibly assist Ambassador Crocker, would be instrumental in assisting with the leadership restructuring of Iraq's military. While ISIL's growth and development is not a surprise and is well documented, the rapid collapse of the Iraq army in Fallujah and Mosul, and in the north in general, was a major surprise. What we did know is that while Maliki was systematically purging his political opponents he was doing much the same to IA leaders, many who had distinguished themselves during the "Surge" in 2007 and 2008. Maliki replaced them with cronies and hacks who over time, because of their incompetence as leaders, drove down the morale of their units, so much so, that in 3 years, some of the units that fled in the face of the ISIL advance were only at 50% strength. Unit cohesion is the glue that binds successful ground units and in these IA units there was none. Additionally, some of the generals fled first, which produced a panic among their subordinates.

Some of what we are doing now to help the IA makes sense, but more can be done. Certainly providing teams to conduct assessment of the IA is essential. The NY Times reported Sunday on some of that assessment to include Sunni informants within the IA, Shia militias who are now part of the IA and about 50% of the IA is capable of receiving advisors. While this is disturbing it is not surprising and confirms what ISW has been reporting for a month. Some will conclude this is a hopeless situation, in fact, it is not. No one should underestimate this tough challenge but US military advisors and planners can assist the IA with the defense of Baghdad to include the Baghdad international airport. Air ground controllers from US Army special forces should be placed in key and selected Iraq units who are vital to the defense, considering the security and risk to those teams. As such, they would assist in employing US attack helicopters and US strike aircraft in a close air support role. Some of the IA units have malign actors in them both Sunni and Shia. Gen. Petraeus could influence an Iraq political decision to remove them. This was successfully done in the past.

U.S. advisors can assist with the reconstruction of IA units that disintegrated along with establishing and overseeing a necessary training program. Finally, if the IA can generate the necessary combat power, U.S. advisors and planners can assist with the plans and execution of a counter offensive to retake lost territory. Air ground controllers and air power should assist the IA ground units. Let me be clear I am not suggesting a return of combat troops to Iraq with the exception of air ground controllers who will be assisting IA ground units and special operations forces who would conduct combat operations against high value targets. Even with these measures there is no certainty that Baghdad will be successfully defended, although it is likely, and there is less certainty that the IA can reconstitute disintegrated units, retrain, and execute a successful counter offense to retake lost territory.

To do nothing more, diplomatically, politically and militarily however, almost guarantees with certainty that the Iraq as the world knew it will be gone with the prospect of ISIL dominating most of the country. Iran and Russia see this upheaval as opportunity to advance their national interests in the region. Russia desires to be a key player in the Middle East and influence other actions as they are doing successfully in Syria and Iran desires Iraq to be a client state similar to Syria. Maliki has brought them in as significant international supporters to assist with operations against ISIL which only enhances Maliki's political position due to the lack of tangible support by the US.

Let me conclude by simply saying this is a time for less handwringing about how we got here and who is at fault and more focus on US resolve to lead a determined effort to push back and eventually defeat ISIL, which should be a part of a larger comprehensive strategy to assist our partners in the region to stop the rise of radical Islam. Iraq needs capable and sophisticated US assistance to reconcile its damaging political differences by moving towards a unity government.

Thank you and I look forward to your questions.

———

Mr. POE. Thank you, General.

Mr. Bandow, you have 5 minutes.

STATEMENT OF MR. DOUG BANDOW, SENIOR FELLOW, CATO INSTITUTE

Mr. BANDOW. Well, thank you, Chairman Poe, Ranking Member Sherman, Chairman Ros-Lehtinen, and Ranking Member Deutch, and other members. I appreciate the opportunity to partipcate in this hearing.

Without doubt, the rise of the Islamic State of Iraq and Levant represents a significant failure for U.S. policy. Although a matter of great concern and quite serious, it does not pose the sort of threat that requires immediate military action, however. The Sunni group ISIL appears to lack the strength necessary to capture Baghdad or take control of the majority Shi'a state, and Syria's ISIL faces multiple political and military challenges as well. It is one thing to declare a caliphate; it is quite another to actually rule.

I think there are a number of lessons to bear in mind as we think about the future. One is that intervention brings unintended consequences, which often are unpredictable and uncontrollable. We certainly found that our policy toward Iraq has always been challenged by the unexpected. That has not changed. Even had a new government in Baghdad been amenable to a continued U.S. military presence, I doubt that would have offered a remedy to the sectarian hostilities that have exploded full force today. We have to bear those kinds of unintended consequences in mind.

America's interest varies depending upon the character of the groups that we are dealing with. In general, a restrained U.S. response emphasizing retaliation with allies taking principal, direct responsiblility is the best approach, I believe.

The question in this case is: What is ISIL? Very different from a guerrilla operation or a militia in a civil war, obviously, or transnational groups such as al-Qaeda, but ISIL's character so far, while not immutable, appears to be more like a party in a traditional civil war, and to the extent that it succeeds in creating a geographic territory, opens itself up to retaliation, and, therefore, has a different incentive structure in terms of how it approaches the United States. That, I would argue, gives the United States an opportunity for a thoughtful and measured response as opposed to a precipitous response.

Indeed, the organization's success so far has depended much on Ba'athist loyalists and tribal leaders more interested in winning regional autonomy or a fair distribution of national spoils than returning to the 7th century. I think that division is one that needs to be exploited, particularly in Baghdad, and that is a particular problem that we have with the current government.

I believe that another lesson we should bear in mind is that U.S. military action almost certainly would result in costs as well as benefits. We have learned so far the limits of American power, especially when imposed from afar with little public support in America for long-term involvement that potentially looks like social engineering.

I believe that airpower, while helpful, is not going to liberate captured cities or turn territory back over to the Sunni—the Shi'a government. And the danger of targeting Sunni areas is killing those who, in fact, worked with the United States back during the surge in opposing al-Qaeda.

The U.S. I believe loses by giving a blank check to Baghdad. The Maliki government is perhaps the primary instrument responsible for the current disaster with the Prime Minister misgoverning, exacerbating sectarian tensions and weakening his own government's governing institutions, particularly the military.

To support that government rewards his strategy. A new government would be best. It is not clear, however, if it is in our power to impose it. He must understand, however, that the reason his country faces crisis is the way that he has governed. But there is a danger for the United States tying itself to his government, particularly if military action is involved, because if we get involved in what is effectively a sectarian war, taking sides there, we may make more enemies than friends.

Moreover, back in Baghdad, we must be careful not to foreclose potential solutions, including some form of federalism or even partition. The Kurds clearly are moving toward a vote toward independence. They are interested in that option. They long have been. The willingness of mainstream Sunnis to back ISIL demonstrates the depth of their alienation there.

It would certainly be best, I believe, to keep Iraq together, but that's not clearly the only option. The U.S. should be discussing with other parties in the region, countries like Jordan, which clearly face serious threats here, and Turkey and others, of how to diffuse the potential sectarian explosion.

I realize the support for the Syrian opposition. However, I fear that backing the Syrian resistance further undermines ultimately the Iraqi Government. And that while the Damascus Government is odious, it is not as obviously inimical to American interests as an ISIL caliphate stretching across the region. To some degree, I believe we have to set priorities here, and I fear that backing the opposition is likely to lead to worse results in terms of ISIL.

Finally, it is critical to involve America's friends and allies. Countries like Turkey, Jordan, Lebanon, and others have an extraordinary amount at stake. The question, then, is how we can involve their potential and their abilities. They vary dramatically, obviously. Nevertheless, they have the most at stake. They are closest to the region. And to the extent they are Muslim nations, they are better positioned than the United States for involvement in what risks being a sectarian conflict.

[The prepared statement of Mr. Bandow follows:]

Testimony of Doug Bandow[1]

House Committee on Foreign Affairs:
Subcommittee on Terrorism, Nonproliferation, and Trade
Subcommittee on the Middle East and North Africa
Hearing on "The Rise of ISIL: Iraq and Beyond"

July 15, 2014

Introduction

Without doubt, the rise of the Islamic State of Iraq and the Levant (ISIL) represents a significant failure of U.S. policy. However, such a reverse was not entirely unexpected. The Iraqi government had exacerbated internal divisions and weakened military forces by placing sectarian and political considerations before good governance. As a result, Baghdad lost control of portions of its territory, most notably the city of Fallujah, months ago. While the seizure of Mosul, Tikrit, and other territory last month came with great suddenness, it reflected problems long in the making.

Although serious, the rise of ISIL does not yet pose the sort of dire, let alone existential, threat to American security requiring dramatic and immediate action. While the government in Baghdad appears ill-prepared to regain its lost territory and suppress the rebels, the Sunni group ISIL appears to lack the strength necessary to capture Baghdad, let alone gain control of majority-Shia nation. In Syria the ISIL radicals face simultaneous military challenges from the government, moderate opposition forces, and even slightly less extreme jihadists, as well as the political task of establishing a functioning government in areas under its control.

Most important, so far, at least, ISIL, unlike al-Qaeda, has not confronted the U.S. To the extent that the group succeeds in creating a traditional government over a defined territory, it will establish a "return address" for retaliation should it seek to strike America. This suggests a more manageable problem at the moment, at least, than that posed by al-Qaeda in 2001.

Of course, Iraq's near collapse still offers a challenge with unpredictable, and certainly negative, consequences for the U.S. But Washington should react circumspectly, avoiding further entanglement where possible in a conflict likely to generate further unintended consequences of potentially significant magnitude.

Lessons from ISIL's Advance

There are a number of lessons to ponder from ISIL's expansion across Syria and particularly into Iraq. They suggest lessons both in developing a short-term response and shaping longer-term strategies.

Intervention brings unintended consequences which often are unpredictable and uncontrollable. Debates over blame and policy alternatives which might have avoided today's situation are interesting but underestimate the inherent problems of intervening in such a region and such a conflict. No doubt, multiple administrations could have acted differently and more competently. But hindsight always is clearer.

---

[1] Doug Bandow is a Senior Fellow at the Cato Institute and a former Special Assistant to President Ronald Reagan.

Those judging a policy such as invading and occupying Iraq should take for granted that some assumptions will be erroneous, some policies will be mistaken, and some outcomes will be unplanned. If the strategy cannot survive the unexpected, its flaws run far deeper. Such an intervention—seeking to transform another society from outside, despite significant differences in history, religion, culture, tradition, ethnicity, interest, and more—inevitably creates a large risk of failure. And such an action almost inevitably will replace one set of problems with another set of equal if not greater magnitude.

Indeed, our experience in the Middle East highlights how one intervention almost always begets another and another. The 1953 coup against Iranian Prime Minister Mohammad Mossadegh elevated the Shah to full power. His authoritarian misrule led to his ouster in 1979. The triumph of Islamic radicals in Tehran caused Washington to back Iraq's Saddam Hussein's aggressive war against Iran. In 1990 Hussein acted as the U.S. had feared the Iranians would act, expanding in the Gulf, leading to the first Gulf War and a force deployment in Saudi Arabia, which Deputy Defense Secretary Paul Wolfowitz later acknowledged to be one of Osama bin Laden's grievances.

The second Gulf War removed Hussein—along with his heavy-handed suppression of sectarian strife and role as counterweight to Iran. Even had the new government in Baghdad been amenable to a continued U.S. military presence, the latter would have offered little remedy for the sectarian hostilities which have exploded with full force today. Developing U.S. policy today requires recognizing the potential of another round of unintended consequences.

Speaking of Iraq's sectarian proclivities, the president recently opined that "old habits die hard." He was correct. However, his sentiment even more accurately applies to Washington's compulsion to intervene militarily all over the world seemingly without regard to long-term consequences.

America's interest varies dramatically based on the character of potential adversary groups such as ISIL. The world is filled with forces representing various degrees of antagonism and hostility toward the U.S., but most have little occasion to act on those sentiments. They may lack the desire, opportunity, or means to strike, or fear the consequences of doing so. The latter—deterrence—kept the most horrid dictatorships of Joseph Stalin's Soviet Union and Mao Zedong's in check for decades. That prospect also is why ugly regimes such as North Korea threaten their neighbors rather than America.

In general, a restrained U.S. response emphasizing the promise of overwhelming retaliation, with allies taking responsibility for more direct contact, is the best approach in such cases. Directly intervening in conflicts without direct impact on America and initiating preventive wars where intentions and capabilities are unclear, as against Hussein's Iraq, usually create bigger problems than those solved. For this reason alone, such interventions should be last resorts.

Very different is the threat posed by transnational groups, such as al-Qaeda, which focus their ire on America and are almost impossible to deter. Although trade-offs remain important—for instance, promiscuous and especially misdirected drone strikes may create more enemies than they kill—the potential for attack against America is higher and the need for preemption (which differs from preventive war) is greater. Enemies planning attacks must be incapacitated, whether killed, captured, or debilitated.

Although ISIL's character is not immutable, so far it acts more like a party in a traditional civil war than a terrorist group. In fact, the organization even offers social services and religious education more characteristic of a traditional government. ISIL's break with al-Qaeda apparently reflected at least in part the latter's focus on the "far enemy," that is, the U.S. In contrast, ISIL wanted to become something akin to a "real country." Which makes it far more dangerous for the governments of Iraq and Syria, in particular, than for America.

To the extent that the organization establishes effective control over a territory, which remains problematic, it will have less incentive to strike the U.S., since doing so would, as with the Taliban in Afghanistan, risk its geopolitical gains. The group continues to pose a serious challenge, and one which could morph into something different and more menacing over time. But today Washington has an opportunity for a considered, restrained, and measured response.

Moreover, Iraq is not likely to fall under ISIL control and become a terrorist state. Although these Islamic radicals, deploying a small but disciplined military force, have been able to grab most of Sunni-dominated Anbar Province, they lack the resources necessary to conquer Iraq or even take Baghdad. The slide toward sectarian strife, exacerbated with ISIL's claims to have executed hundreds of Sunni soldiers, will strengthen popular Shiite resistance.

Moreover, the organization's success so far has depended on Baathist loyalists and tribal leaders more interested in winning regional autonomy and a fairer distribution of national spoils than in returning to the 7th century. The group's ostentatious brutality, apparently another factor in its break with al-Qaeda, also is likely to engender resistance. Some clashes already have been reported and the prospect for permanent and stable Islamist rule is uncertain.

U.S. military action almost certainly would result in more costs than benefits. Into this violent and unpredictable imbroglio President Obama is sending some Special Forces and contemplating "targeted, precise military action," presumably air and drone strikes. Some observers have called for confronting not just ISIL, but also the Baghdad government to force it to broaden its support and demobilize Shiite militias, and Tehran, to limit the latter's influence and compel the withdrawal of any military units.

Unfortunately, Washington already has learned the limits of military power, especially when imposed from afar with little popular support for long-term occupation in pursuit of what amounts to international social engineering. The more the U.S. attempts to do, the less likely it will do it well. Iraq's most serious problem today is that the state lacks credibility and will, and the military lacks leadership and commitment. These America cannot provide.

Military action is even more problematic. Most tempting may be limited drone strikes against ISIL's leadership, but such a campaign would require accurate intelligence. Moreover, the killing of the leaders of ISIL's earlier incarnations did not break the group or stop its activities. Today ISIL is too big to simply decapitate.

Nor does a broader use of airpower offer an easy solution. The allies employed some 25,000 strikes on behalf of highly-motivated opposition forces in Libya and the latter still took several months to triumph in a desert-oriented campaign. Air attacks have limited effectiveness in urban warfare and cannot liberate captured cities. To restrict "collateral damage" airpower best relies on ground support for targeting, something that could not be left to frankly untrustworthy sectarian Iraqi forces. Unfortunately, targeting Sunni areas almost inevitably would mean killing people, including noncombatants, once allied with Washington against al-Qaeda—as part of the "Sunni awakening" which was the key to the success of the Bush "surge." Turning former Sunni allies into enemies would put America's future position at risk while encouraging terrorism from another direction. The U.S. cannot escape blowback if it joins another Mideast conflict.

America loses by giving a blank check to Baghdad or attempting to transform Baghdad. Next to ISIL's Abu Bakr al-Baghdadi, the man most responsible for the ongoing debacle is Iraqi Prime Minister Nouri al-Maliki. The latter has misgoverned, exacerbated sectarian tensions, and weakened his nation's governing institutions. To support his government is to reward his counterproductive behavior and encourage continuation of a strategy which has brought his country to near ruin. The tighter the U.S. embrace, the less likely he will either reform his government or reach beyond his narrow Shia base of support.

Moreover, tying America to his government would prove particularly dangerous if the conflict turns into a sectarian war. ISIL's atrocities and threats have galvanized Iraq's Shia majority, with young men joining the military and Shiite militias cooperating with security forces. The result looks likely to become a bitter and potentially long struggle between essentially lawless paramilitaries rather than a decisive conventional campaign by conventional forces. Washington does not want to be drawn into such a conflict.

Indeed, as noted earlier, ISIL has succeeded to its current degree in Iraq because it has won support from former Baathists and Sunni tribes. Some of the latter worked with America as part of the Sunni Awakening. At the latter's height tens of thousands of Sunnis were working with the U.S. against al-Qaeda and other foreign jihadists. The U.S. might deplore their cooperation with ISIL today, but they have done so for reasons entirely unconnected to America. They are not and must not be turned into America's enemies.

For understandable reasons the administration has been working to oust Maliki in favor of a more pliant and inclusive leader. Unfortunately, this effort is unlikely to turn out well. If unsuccessful, future cooperation with Baghdad will be made more difficult. Yet this is not the first U.S. attempt to get Maliki to be more responsible, and he so far has successfully resisted U.S., as well as domestic, pressure. His spokesman publicly called for support rather than pressure from Washington. As much as other Iraqis may want to replace him, they are less likely to act under American duress, especially while their nation faces a potentially existential threat.

Even if Washington's efforts turned out to be successful, Maliki's replacement might not be much better. Talk of Ahmed Chalabi, for instance, gives no cause for confidence. And Washington would be tied to "its man" for good or ill. Maliki illustrates that downside.

Moreover, appearing to reflexively back Baghdad risks foreclosing potential solutions, including some form of federalism or even partition. The Iraqi Humpty Dumpty has fallen off of the wall. The Kurds are moving toward a vote over independence. The willingness of mainstream Sunnis to back ISIL demonstrates the depth of their alienation from Baghdad. The collapse of the Iraqi military suggests that the national government is unlikely to quickly reassert its authority. The U.S. and other interested parties, including Jordan, Israel, Turkey, and Iran should be talking informally and quietly about options to defuse the potential sectarian explosion. While Washington could help advance such an approach, no plan will succeed without support of regional states and local peoples. All options should be in play.

Backing the Syrian resistance against Bashar al-Assad's government risks further undermining the Iraqi government and ultimately American interests. The civil war in Syria obviously is a humanitarian tragedy, but it long has been well beyond Washington's control. The claim that if only the U.S. had given the right measure of support to the right group at the right time a democratic government representing all Syrians would have emerged is dubious: little about American involvement in the Middle East suggests the necessary combination of perspicacity, nuance, competence, and humility. In any case, the conflict has moved well beyond any such moment.

The Damascus government is odious, but not as obviously inimical to U.S. interests as an ISIL "caliphate" reaching across Iraq and Syria. Further weakening the Assad regime increases the opening for ISIL and other jihadist forces. While aiding more moderate fighters might help them regain lost ground against radical forces, experience suggest doing so is more likely to create a new source of materiel resupply for ISIL—if the latter continues to triumph in clashes between the two. (Already the group has captured a wealth of U.S. weapons, including Blackhawk helicopters!) The U.S. risks being too clever by half, presuming that it can control the outcome of a war that so far has proved as unpredictable as any other in the Mideast.

Ultimately, Washington must set priorities. The overthrow of Assad is desirable in theory but, like the ouster of Hussein, may yield unexpectedly bloody consequences in practice. One likely result would include further strengthening ISIL, a more clear and present danger than Assad. Attempting to play both sides, helping the government battling jihadist extremists in Iraq while opposing the government fulfilling the same role in Syria, risks dual failure.

ISIL is more a problem for America's friends and allies than for America. To the extent that the group remains an aspirant to national power rather than an advocate of terror against the U.S., it most directly threatens countries in the region. These states, overwhelmingly Muslim other than Israel and Lebanon, possess greater credibility in confronting a group claiming to represent Islam. Washington should expect these nations to respond to the threat.

Unfortunately, American officials seem reluctant to relinquish control, despite their evident and longstanding difficulty in shaping geopolitical circumstances to advance U.S. ends. Given the costs of action, it makes more sense to expect the nations with the most at stake to be most responsible. The outcome may not be precisely to Washington's liking, but it isn't likely to be so even with more direct American intervention.

Multiple actors are interested in ISIL, which has claimed territory as far as Kuwait, Israel, and Turkey. First and most important is Iraq. The best hope for creating a more responsible and unifying government comes from the threat posed by ISIL. Indeed, the most obvious strategy for ending the danger of a "caliphate" is weaning away the group's Sunni allies. They must come to see greater benefits in cooperating with a reformed government in Baghdad than in reconstructing an ancient caliphate.

Second is Iran. Washington's reluctance to countenance Tehran's involvement in Iraq is understandable but irrelevant. Hussein's loss always was going to be Iran's gain, the Bush administration's intentions notwithstanding. There is nothing Washington can do to change that today. The more America is willing to tie itself to the Maliki government the less the latter might need to rely on Iran, but the impact likely would be marginal. The overwhelming religious, cultural, personal, economic, and geopolitical ties would remain. The U.S. always will be a distant and alien power. Under these circumstances, it would be better to have Iran rather than America deeply involved in Iraq what may end up as a barely disguised sectarian conflict.

Third is Turkey. Recent events, such as ISIL's capture of Turkish diplomats and truck drivers, have tempered Ankara's enthusiasm for overthrowing the Assad regime. Turkey is a Muslim nation with significant military capabilities which borders both Iraq and Syria. No doubt, the Erdogan government would find military involvement in the current struggle discomfiting, and Baghdad might be little more enthusiastic. However, from America's standpoint U.S. military involvement would be far worse.

Fourth is Saudi Arabia (and other Gulf States). Although not directly involved in the fighting, Riyadh has been funding and arming opposition forces in Syria. Washington cannot expect independent nations, even friendly ones, to automatically follow U.S. policy, but it should emphasize that any aid to radical groups such as ISIL is highly counterproductive. The group already has multiple sources of funding, most not subject to U.S. pressure. However, states claiming to be friendly to America should not be adding to its financial or military resources, especially nations which look to the U.S. for their defense.

Fifth, other countries, including Israel, Jordan, and Lebanon, have an interest in rolling back ISIL's gains. They all have different capabilities, and the implications of their involvement vary dramatically. However, Washington should be burning the diplomatic wires to encourage them to take action according to their interests and abilities. The U.S. has enough challenges in the Middle East and elsewhere around the world to jump into another conflict.

The U.S. should downplay Iran's involvement in Iraq since there is little Washington can do to prevent or limit it. Tehran's role in Iraq has caused great discomfort, but that was inevitable once the Bush administration removed Hussein from power. Although as I noted earlier American policy might have some impact at the margin on the degree of Iranian influence, the natural connections between the two Shia-majority nations always will outrange Baghdad's relations with Washington, especially as long as the U.S. is at odds with Tehran.

Rather than verbalize its unease and thus demonstrate its impotence, or engage in high level talks and ratify Iran's role, the Obama administration should quietly ensure that any U.S. military involvement does not clash with actions taken by Tehran. America's role should remain advisory, at most, but it would be best to ensure no inadvertent complications. The crisis in Iraq has placed a greater premium on improving relations with Iran—and especially resolving the nuclear issue, if possible. However, it would be a mistake to link the issues since Tehran's nuclear status remains the most critical bilateral challenge for Washington (as well as of great interest to allied states, including in Europe, and Persian Gulf, and Israel), and a successful, peaceful resolution, however unlikely it might appear at this point, would open the door to resolving or moderating other disputes.

Suggested Approach to Iraq

Rather than engage in a well-publicized argument over relative blame of the past two administrations, U.S. policymakers should emphasize that the greatest fault, other than of Baghdadi and ISIL's other practiced killers, lies with the Iraqis. Having sown the wind, the Maliki government now is reaping the whirlwind. Thus, Washington should continue to place responsibility on the Iraqi government to adopt a more inclusive political approach, including discussions of a more federal government structure.

The U.S. also should promote a better coordinated regional approach by the many states affected by ISIL's rise. Far better that Muslim nations challenge Muslim radicals than American forces do so. Washington's interests in the Iraqi meltdown are real, but not nearly as serious as those of surrounding countries.

The Obama administration should rethink the advisability of further involvement in the Syrian civil war. A vision of the unlikely perfect, the replacement of the Assad regime with a liberal, democratic opposition, should not become the enemy of the more realistic good, a negotiated compromise limiting the power of radicals such as ISIL. The spillover into Iraq has become a prime consideration.

Finally, Washington should limit its involvement where the threat remains indirect. ISIL is a bad actor, but not yet one warranting a direct American military response. Recent experience in the region and beyond demonstrates that war should be a last resort. ISIL has grown most obviously out of past U.S. policy mistakes. Washington cannot afford a repeat experience.

Mr. POE. Thank you.

Mr. Eisenstadt, 5 minutes, please, sir.

STATEMENT OF MR. MICHAEL EISENSTADT, SENIOR FELLOW AND DIRECTOR OF THE MILITARY AND SECURITY STUDIES PROGRAM, THE WASHINGTON INSTITUTE FOR NEAR EAST POLICY

Mr. EISENSTADT. Chairman Poe, Ranking Member Sherman, Chairman Ros-Lehtinen, and Ranking Member Deutch, and other members, thank you for giving me the opportunity to testify before your committee about this pressing issue.

The rapid capture of large swaths of northern Iraq last month by ISIL has altered the strategic landscape of the Middle East. Given the amounts of blood and treasury the United States has already invested in Iraq, why should Americans care? Simply because the United States still has vital security interests that are affected greatly by developments in Iraq and the region. And these interests are: One, combating terrorism and the potential threat this poses to the American homeland; two, oil; three, nonproliferation; and, four, continuous Iranian influence.

Iraq is where nearly all of these issues converge. Iraq is now a potential springboard for ISIL subversion directed against Jordan and Saudi Arabia, and for ISIL terrorist attacks outside the region. It is an oil producer that was, at least until recently, expected to account for 45 percent of all future growth in world oil supplies in the coming years. And Iraq is the land bridge that enables Iran to more easily project influence in the Levant.

First, developments in Iraq have the potential to shape vital U.S. security interests in the Middle East and perhaps even the security of the homeland in the coming years. And the experience of the past decade teaches us that for this reason it is vitally important for the U.S. to try to influence the course and outcome of developments in that still-important region. Experience shows that if you don't visit the Middle East, the Middle East will visit you.

So what is next? ISIL is not likely to replicate its spectacular military achievements in the Baghdad area, yet the Iraqi security forces were seen by many locals in northern Iraq as an army of occupation. In Baghdad, they are defending home turf and can rely on the support of thousands of shared militiamen mobilized to fight ISIL. Indeed, the latter's efforts to move on Baghdad, at least for now, have stalled.

The conflict has effectively settled into what is likely to be a prolonged and bloody war of attrition. There will be no more easy victories for ISIL, though its ability to wreak havoc in the capital and elsewhere, through suicide bombings and sectarian killings, remains undiminished. That said, we must not be complacent because it appears that the momentum of the ISIL advance has been broken. That could change very quickly.

Neither will it be easy for the Iraqi security forces to reclaim many of the areas that were lost to ISIL. The ISF has been trying to do so in Fallujah for months now without success, even though that city is a mere 25 or so miles west of Baghdad. For the ISF to succeed, it will need to find allies among the Sunnis in order to reprise the tribal uprising that helped defeat al-Qaeda in Iraq in 2006 and 2007.

But having been used and abandoned once before, and targeted by both government forces and al-Qaeda since, the Sunni tribes won't come around so easily this time. ISIL also faces challenges. It is spread thin throughout northern Iraq. If it is to hang on to its territorial gains, it will have to hold together the loose military coalition that it leads, which includes Ba'athist insurgent groups and tribal militias whose interests diverge from those of ISIL.

It will have to avoid the tendency to alienate the very Sunni constituency it claims to represent by its harsh application of Islamic law. And it will face the challenge of having been transformed virtually overnight from perhaps the world's wealthiest terrorist group to one of the world's poorest de facto states. These dynamics will create opportunities for the al-Maliki government, or its successor, if it is wise enough to seize upon them.

So what should the U.S. do? First, don't intervene directly in Iraq civil war, at least not yet. Instead, the U.S. should continue quietly providing intelligence, advice, and munitions to the Iraqi security forces, but it should slow roll the delivery of large advanced systems such as Apache helicopters and F–16 fighters, which Iraq currently lacks the pilots to fly anyhow.

Just thinking about more significant support, to include U.S. joining air strikes, will come only if the Prime Minister takes a different politic tack toward the country's Sunni Arabs and Kurds. This will maximize U.S. leverage at this crucial time in the government formation process, in order to achieve a political outcome that could pave the way for a truly effective military campaign against ISIL, one that reprises the Sunni Arab tribal uprisings of 2006 and 2007.

Right now, politics in Baghdad do not permit such campaign. Except to defend Baghdad, the U.S. should, therefore, issue kinetic action until the Iraqis get the politics piece right.

Two, we should start to talk about working with Iran against ISIL. The enemy of our enemy is not necessarily our friend. The U.S. and Iran have a common enemy in ISIL, but the interests of the two are not aligned, whether regarding U.S. influence in Iraq, the nature of Iraqi politics, on the issue of Prime Minister Maliki, and the role of sectarian militias in combating ISIL. And such talk only feeds speculation that Washington and Tehran are conspiring at the expense of the Sunnis, and that the United States believes that the way to fight Sunni jihadists is by allying with Shi'ite jihadists.

Finally, train and equip the moderate Syrian opposition to pressure ISIL and Iraq. ISIL has a major presence in eastern Syria, and it is important to put pressure on it there, especially in light of its recent gains in Iraq. Revitalizing the moderate opposition will constitute a challenge to ISIL, but it could force the latter to redeploy at least some of its forces from Iraq to secure its Syrian sanctuary, thereby relieving some of the pressure on the Maliki government and perhaps loosening its hold on the newly taken ground in Iraq. This will take time, however, and the hour is late. We must move quickly.

Thank you.

[The prepared statement of Mr. Eisenstadt follows:]

Managing the Crisis in Iraq

Michael Eisenstadt
Senior Fellow and Director, Military and Security Studies Program
The Washington Institute for Near East Policy

Testimony submitted to the United States House of Representatives
Subcommittees on Terrorism, Nonproliferation, and Trade and the Middle East and North Africa
July 15, 2014

The rapid capture of large swathes of northern Iraq last month by a relatively small, lightly armed force of Sunni Arab militants fighting under the banner of the Islamic State in Iraq and the Levant (ISIL)—now known as the Islamic State (IS)—has altered the strategic landscape of the Middle East. The successor to al-Qaida in Iraq, IS has ridden a wave of resentment felt by Iraq's Sunni Arabs at the exclusionary, sectarian policies pursued by Iraq's Shiite Prime Minister Nouri al-Maliki.

The rise of IS was greatly facilitated by Syria's civil war, which enabled it to establish a base of operations in eastern Syria and to transform itself into a lightly armed, mobile force with thousands of experienced fighters (including thousands of freed prisoners and foreign volunteers). Over a year ago, IS began shifting resources back to Iraq, operating openly in the western part of the country, launching a suicide bombing campaign focused on Baghdad that heralded its return, and early this year seizing control of several towns in Anbar province, including Fallujah.[1]

The IS capture of Mosul and large parts of northern Iraq, then, is part of a multi-phased plan to establish an Islamic state that extends from Lebanon to Iraq. The next big target for IS is Baghdad.

But IS is not likely to replicate these spectacular military achievements in the Baghdad area. If the Iraqi Security Forces (ISF) were seen by many locals in northern Iraq as an army of occupation, in Baghdad it is defending home turf and it can rely on the support of thousands of Shiite militiamen that have been mobilized to fight IS, as well as most of the population. Despite a number of additional gains since the fall of Mosul (Tel Afar, al-Qaim, and Tikrit, among others), IS's efforts to take the cities of Samarra and Baquba, north and northeast of Baghdad, respectively, and to move on the capital, seem to have stalled.

The conflict has effectively settled into what is likely to be a prolonged and bloody war of attrition. There will be no more easy victories for IS, though its ability to wreak havoc in the capital and elsewhere through suicide bombings and sectarian killings remains undiminished.

Neither will it be easy for the ISF to reclaim many of the areas that were lost to IS. It has been trying to do so in Fallujah for months now, without success—even though that city is a mere 25 miles west of Baghdad. For the ISF to succeed, it will need to find allies among the Sunnis, to reprise the tribal uprising that helped defeat al-Qaida in Iraq in 2006-2007. But having been used and abandoned once before, and targeted by both government forces and al-Qaida since, the tribes won't come around so easily this time.

IS also faces challenges. It is spread thin throughout northern Iraq. If it is to hang onto its territorial gains, it will have to hold together the loose military coalition that it leads, which includes Baathist insurgent groups and tribal militias whose interests diverge from those of IS. This won't be easy. And it will have to avoid the tendency to alienate the very Sunni constituency it claims to represent by its harsh application of Islamic law. These dynamics will create opportunities for the al-Maliki government (or its successor) if it is smart enough to seize them.

---

[1] *Threat Posed by the Islamic State of Iraq and the Levant (ISIL)*, Testimony of Deputy Assistant Secretary Brett McGurk, House Foreign Affairs Committee Hearing: Iraq, February 5, 2014, http://docs.house.gov/meetings/FA/FA00/20140205/101716/HHRG-113-FA00-Wstate-McGurkB-20140205.pdf; *The Resurgence of Al-Qaeda in Iraq*, Testimony of Michael Knights, House Committee on Foreign Affairs, Subcommittee on Terrorism, Non-Proliferation and Trade, and Subcommittee on the Middle East and North Africa, December 12, 2013, http://www.washingtoninstitute.org/uploads/Documents/testimony/KnightsTestimony20131212.pdf.

Given how much blood and treasure the United States has already invested in Iraq (nearly 4,500 killed, more than 30,000 wounded, and well over $1 trillion spent), why should Americans care about what is going on there now? Simply because, 'if you do not visit the Middle East, it will visit you.' The U.S. experience in the region since its forces withdrew from Iraq in 2011 shows that the United States needs to shape and influence developments in the region—to the degree it is able to do so—as vital U.S. security interests are affected by what happens there.

What are these interests? They are: 1) containing terrorist threats; 2) oil; 3) nonproliferation, and; 4) preventing the emergence of a regional hegemon.

Containing terrorist threats: civil wars in Iraq (2006-2007, 2014-present) and Syria (2011-present) have been major catalysts for the sectarian polarization of the region and the radicalization of Muslims worldwide, through the formulation and export of radical Islamic doctrines and the mobilization of fighters from around the world to participate in these conflicts. The Syrian civil war in particular has attracted thousands of foreign fighters who will almost certainly wreak havoc when they return home. And Iraq is now the place where all these developments converge, as the seat of a radical Islamic 'caliphate' that is likely to become a springboard for aggression against Jordan and Saudi Arabia and for terrorist attacks around the world.

Oil: despite the fact that Persian Gulf oil accounts for less than 30% of U.S. petroleum imports, and that imported oil accounts for only 40% of total U.S. petroleum consumption (a proportion that is likely to decline further due to the U.S. shale oil revolution), Middle Eastern oil—which accounts for about half of the world's oil and gas reserves—is still critical to the world economy. Iraq, moreover, was until recently expected to account for 45% of all future growth in world oil supplies. Thus, Iraqi oil in particular and Middle Eastern oil in general, are still critical to the health of the U.S. and world economies, though renewed conflict means that Iraqi oil is unlikely to meet previous growth projections.[2]

Nonproliferation: while the Middle East has seen a number of positive proliferation trends in recent years with the dismantling or destruction of the known weapons of mass destruction (WMD) programs of Iraq, Libya, and Syria, developments in the region will very much influence the future of the global nuclear nonproliferation regime. Even if Iran accepts long-term caps on its nuclear program, its status as a nuclear threshold state could be sufficient to spur a nuclear cascade in an unstable region wracked by political violence and terrorism. (The crisis prompted by Syria's use of chemical weapons and concerns that this stockpile could fall into the hands of terrorists have demonstrated the dangers posed by WMD in a region convulsed by unrest.) Yet, IS's recent successes could make Iran even less amenable to accepting constraints on its nuclear program.

Preventing a regional hegemon: the U.S. tilted toward Iraq during the latter's war with Iran in the 1980s and it went to war with Iraq in 1991, to prevent either Iraq or Iran from becoming a regional hegemon and dominating the world's oil supply. Preventing the emergence of a regional hegemon remains a vital U.S. interest, yet the administration's policies in Syria and Iraq have contributed to the consolidation of a pro-Iranian bloc (the so-called 'axis of resistance') that stretches from the Levant to the Gulf, and that has been a primary driver of sectarian polarization and instability in the region. By dint of geography, Iraq is a land bridge that can facilitate or hinder Iran's efforts to project influence in the Levant; accordingly, preventing the full integration of Iraq into the 'axis of resistance' remains a vital U.S. interest. This will take an active effort on the part of the United States. One thing that Washington should have learned from the experience of recent years, is that contrary to the conventional wisdom popular in some circles, Iranian influence in Iraq and the region is *not* 'self-limiting,' and must be actively countered.[3]

Thus, Iraq has the potential to have a major impact on U.S. security interest in the Middle East in the coming years. Given these realities, the United States should respond to the threats posed to these interests by recent events in Iraq by pursuing several objectives:

---

[2] Meghan L.O'Sullivan, "Future of Oil Hangs on Iraqi Politics," *Bloomberg View*, July 9, 2014, http://www.bloombergview.com/articles/2014-07-09/future-of-oil-hangs-on-iraqi-politics.
[3] Vali Nasr, "Why Contain Iran When Its Own Aims Will Do Just That?" *Bloomberg View*, October 31, 2011, http://www.bloombergview.com/articles/2011-10-31/why-contain-iran-when-its-own-aims-will-do-just-that-vali-nasr.

- Contain, then roll-back IS—though this will not be easy and will take time;
- Limit Iranian influence wherever possible, while cooperating with Tehran when it serves U.S. interests;
- Press Prime Minister Maliki (or his successor) to accept a cross-sectarian power sharing formula to reduce instability, and;
- Pursue indirect approaches to containing IS and undermining the 'axis of resistance' via Syria.

Given the lack of popular support in the United States for military intervention in the Middle East,[4] and the seemingly intractable nature of the problems that the United States faces in the region—which can perhaps be managed, but not solved (at least not anytime soon)—this translates to a policy consisting of the following elements:

Don't over-react and don't intervene—at least not yet. By all appearances, ISF and the sectarian militias fighting by its side have stabilized the battlefield and are keeping IS at bay—at least for now. The U.S. should continue quietly providing intelligence and advice to the ISF, and keep the forces it has recently deployed to the region to provide military options (including 300 military advisors to help the ISF, 500 personnel to secure the embassy and airport, reconnaissance and armed drones and Apache attack helicopters in Baghdad, and the Bataan Amphibious Ready Group in the Persian Gulf).

But the United States should not intervene militarily in this nascent civil war—at least not yet. As long as Nouri al-Maliki continues with his past policies, force should be used only if the U.S. embassy in Baghdad is threatened by IS and its allies. The last thing the U.S. needs is to become an active participant in this fight. Extremists often rely on their enemies overreacting. Direct U.S. intervention in the fighting in the mixed areas in Baghdad, Diyala, Babil, and Salah al-Din provinces could be a recruiting windfall for IS overseas. Don't grant it this favor.

And while the U.S. should expedite the delivery of Hellfire missiles, it should slow-roll the delivery of large, advanced systems, such as Apache helicopters and F-16 fighters (which Iraq currently lacks the pilots to fly anyhow) to signal that more significant support will come only if the Prime Minister takes a different political tack toward the Sunni Arabs and Kurds, whom he has gratuitously antagonized time and again—most recently in the past week.[5]

Thus, the U.S. should allow Prime Minister Maliki to twist in the wind as long as he is not willing to work to achieve a cross-sectarian coalition government, while quietly pushing for an alternative to him who would be willing to work on that basis. It should, however, hold out the prospect of expedited weapons deliveries, and even U.S. drone and air strikes against IS positions in Sunni-only areas in the north as an incentive.

The United States risks marginalizing itself by adopting such a policy of restraint, and for that reason, the United States should continue to provide intelligence and advice so as to not completely sever ties with the ISF, and to give the Iraqi government a taste of what it can expect in abundance if it were to change its ways. But it also maximizes U.S. leverage at this crucial time in the government formation process in order to achieve a political outcome that could pave the way for a truly effective military campaign against IS. At any rate, it is preferable to enabling a sectarian conflict and being seen as complicit in the barrel-bombing of towns like Falluja.

Continue to press Prime Minister Maliki (or his successor) to ally with Sunnis opposed to IS, to reprise the coalition that defeated al-Qaida in Iraq in 2006-2007. During this crisis, al-Maliki has shown that his instinctive response is to play the sectarian card, calling on Shiite militias to rally to the side of the ISF against IS. While that may yield short-term political dividends, in the long run it is a losing bet. The United States should therefore condition the expedited delivery of major weapons systems on his reviving a cross-sectarian strategy—but it should have no illusions that these efforts will succeed, or that al-Maliki will not abandon this strategy once he has achieved his goals (as he has done in the past). Because this strategy is unlikely to succeed, given Maliki's personal and political instincts, the U.S. should simultaneously explore other paths to defeating IS.

[4] Public Sees U.S. Power Declining as Support for Global Engagement Slips, *Pew Research Center*, December 3, 2013, http://www.people-press.org/2013/12/03/public-sees-u-s-power-declining-as-support-for-global-engagement-slips/.
[5] Borzou Daragahi, "Iraq's Maliki blasts Kurds in hard-hitting speech," *Financial Times*, July 9, 2014, http://www.ft.com/cms/s/0/dc1953ac-076d-11e4-81c6-00144feab7de.html#axzz37NxFn3GV.

IS has exploitable vulnerabilities that will likely become manifest in the coming weeks and months. Its recent rapid gains were the result of the collapse, rather than the military defeat of the ISF. (This was the very problem that complicated swift U.S. military victories in Afghanistan in 2001 and Iraq in 2003, and that made the occupation of these countries so difficult. As the U.S. learned in both cases, the hard part is what comes after victory when one hasn't defeated the enemy in detail.) As a result, many soldiers and police fled south to Baghdad or east to the KRG, and at least some of those who survived are likely to fight another day—if they are not arrested for desertion.[6]

Moreover, the coalition IS leads is inherently unstable, with former Bathists, Naqshabandis, and tribal militias likely to eventually bridle against the rule of extreme Islamists who have relied heavily on foreigners for so much of their muscle. There are already signs of tension in the IS military coalition, with IS trying to marginalize its partners in some places (arresting former military officers and Bathists), and clashing with Naqshabandi elements in others. Furthermore, the degree of control it asserts in many areas is unclear. And while IS has been ruling with a light touch thus far, its aforementioned tendency to alienate the constituency it claims to represent is likely to eventually reassert itself, creating options in the future. Indeed, there are already signs that IS is reverting to form in this regard.[7]

IS may well have bitten off more than it can chew. In areas it has 'liberated,' reports abound of rampant unemployment and the collapse of services (water, electricity, and trash collection). And thanks to its rapid success, IS was transformed overnight from perhaps the richest terrorist group in the world, to one of the poorest (*de facto*) states in the world.[8] Even if it is true that it purloined $425 million from Mosul's Central Bank, that it earns $1 million a day from oil smuggling in Iraq, and that it earns income from producing and selling oil in eastern Syria, it probably is not earning anywhere near enough to provide for the ten to fifteen percent of the country's population that it may now control. (By comparison, the Kurdistan Regional Government's budget has been perhaps $12 billion a year, for a roughly comparable population.) This is likely to result in discontent with IS rule in areas that it controls.[9]

Stop the talk about working with Iran against IS. Such talk only feeds speculation that Washington and Tehran are conspiring at the expense of the Sunnis, and that the United States believes that the way to fight Sunni jihadists is by allying with Shiite jihadists. This perception will only further complicate the already polarized and fraught situation in Iraq, and foster additional distrust toward the United States among its traditional (Sunni) Arab allies, at a time that it needs their help in finding a middle way in both Syria and Iraq.

The enemy of our enemy is not necessarily our friend. The United States and Iran have a common enemy in IS, but the interests of the two are not aligned. The United States wants to retain influence in Baghdad, and to create a broad-based government built on cross-sectarian alliances that include the Sunnis as full participants. Iran wants to eliminate U.S. influence in Iraq and ensure that any government formalizes Shiite primacy and Kurdish participation—so that the Kurds have a stake in a unified Iraq and do not seek independence (a move that could influence Iran's own Kurdish minority). But Iran's support for Maliki and his divisive policies have jeopardized these efforts.

Iran has not resolved this contradiction at the heart of its policy, and if it were to eventually decide that Maliki must go (its support for him is not unconditional—he was not its preferred candidate in 2010), there might be a basis to

---

[6] Mike Giglio, "Fear Of ISIS Drives Iraqi Soldiers Into Desertion And Hiding," *BuzzFeed*, June 23, 2014, http://www.buzzfeed.com/mikegiglio/fear-of-isis-drives-iraqi-soldiers-into-desertion-and-hiding; Yasir Abbas and Dan Trombly, "Inside the Collapse of the Iraqi Army's 2nd Division," *War on the Rocks*, July 1, 2014, http://warontherocks.com/2014/07/inside-the-collapse-of-the-iraqi-armys-2nd-division/; Alexander Dziadosz, "Bruised Iraqi army leans on Shi'ite militias, volunteers," *Reuters*, July 10, 2014, http://www.reuters.com/article/2014/07/10/us-iraq-security-volunteers-insight-idUSKBN0FF1IO20140710.
[7] Matt Bradley and Bill Spindle, "Unlikely Allies Aid Militants in Iraq," *Wall Street Journal*, June 16, 2014, http://online.wsj.com/articles/unlikely-1402962546; Hugh Naylor, "Signs of strain in militant ranks as ISIL alienates allies," *The National*, June 21, 2014, http://www.thenational.ae/world/iraq/signs-of-strain-in-militant-ranks-as-isil-alienates-allies; Maggie Fick, Ahmed Rasheed, et al, "Islamic State rounds up ex-Baathists to eliminate potential rivals in Iraq's Mosul," *Reuters*, July 8, 2014, http://uk.reuters.com/article/2014/07/08/uk-iraq-islamic-state-mosul-idUKKBN0FD1AA20140708; Ronen Zeidel, *How ISIS Controls the Occupied Areas in Iraq*, Tel Aviv Notes, vol. 8, no. 13, July 11, 2014, http://www.dayan.org/sites/default/files/Ronen_Zeidel_How_ISIS_Controls_Occupied_Areas_In_Iraq_11072014.pdf.
[8] Personal correspondence with Michael Knights, July 2014.
[9] "Inside Mosul: No Fuel, No Power in a City Under Siege," *Niqash*, June 18, 2014, http://www.niqash.org/articles/?id=3466; Shalaw Mohammed, "Visiting Hawija, a Town Controlled by ISIS Extremists," June 27, 2014, http://www.niqash.org/articles/?id=3478.

work with Iran, at least in principle, to find an acceptable alternative. But Iran is not there yet.[10] And Iran enjoys a number of advantages (particularly its close ties to Iraq's Shiite parties) that ensure it will play a much more important role in the government formation process than will the United States. However, to the degree that many Iraqi parties do not want to be completely beholden to Iran, and that only Washington can deliver the arms and even the military muscle needed to defeat IS—in the form of U.S. drone and air strikes—there still is a (behind-the-scenes) role for the United States to play in the government formation process.

IS's defeat of the ISF was also a major setback for Iran. And IS's rise threatens the so-called 'axis of resistance,' from the Levant to Iran, as IS is active in Lebanon, Syria, Iraq, and its recent victories might inspire violent Salafists already active in Iran.[11] This is yet another reason, barring any major change in policy by Baghdad, not to move too quickly to lavish military support on the Iraqi government, as it is worth letting Tehran consider how its own policies have contributed to the current state of affairs there.

Finally, if the powers that be in Baghdad eventually settle on an alternative to Maliki and form some kind of cross-sectarian government, the United States should make long-term U.S. assistance for rebuilding the ISF conditional on the demobilization of the Shiite sectarian militias, and not their incorporation into the ISF—as happened between 2003-2008. These militias are Tehran's preferred approach for dealing with IS and serve as vectors of Iranian influence, and are sure to have a deleterious impact on Iraqi politics if allowed to remain in place after the current crisis passes (if it passes), and on the professionalism of the security forces if folded into the ISF.[12]

Rebuilding the ISF will prove a formidable task. Prime Minister Maliki remade the ISF in his own image—re-staffing its upper ranks with cronies and rewiring its organizational charts to serve his own purposes. In this sense, it is an extension of his person. It could take years to undo the damage he has done and for a new commander-in-chief to assert control over the ISF. The entire effort to rebuild the ISF will therefore be doomed from the start if the politics aren't right this time.

The road to liberating Iraq passes through Syria. IS has a major presence in eastern Syria and it is important to put pressure on it there, especially in light of its recent gains, which include quantities of arms taken from the ISF. The Obama administration has long debated whether to train and equip the moderate opposition in Syria, and it recently decided to ask Congress for $500 million to fund such an effort—which is more important now than ever before. The revitalization of the moderate opposition will constitute a challenge to IS that could force the latter to redeploy at least some of its forces in Iraq to secure its Syrian sanctuary, thereby relieving some of the pressure on the al-Maliki government, and perhaps loosening IS's hold on ground recently taken, enabling disenchanted elements in Iraq to shake loose of its grip. (It will also enable the moderate Syrian opposition to keep up the pressure on the Assad regime at a time that the latter's allies from various Iraqi Shiite militias have been called home to fight IS.) All this will take time, however, as what is required is not just a train-and-equip effort to enhance the moderate opposition's military capabilities, but the purging of corrupt and criminal elements from the ranks of these groups, and the creation of an effective opposition political organization. There is no time to waste.[13]

[10] Jay Solomon, "Iran's Leaders Split Over Support for Iraq's Maliki," *Wall Street Journal Blog*, July 7, 2014, http://blogs.wsj.com/washwire/2014/07/07/irans-leaders-split-over-support-for-iraqs-maliki/.

[11] Mehdi Khalaji, *Salafism as a National Security Threat for Iran*, Washington Institute Policy Watch 2211, February 20, 2014, http://www.washingtoninstitute.org/policy-analysis/view/salafism-as-a-national-security-threat-for-iran.

[12] Thus, Revolutionary Guard commander Brigadier General Massoud Jazayeri recently stated that Iran "is ready to provide (Iraq) with... the same winning strategy used in Syria to put the terrorists on the defensive... (which) is now taking shape in Iraq—mobilizing masses of all ethnic groups." Mehrdad Balali, "Iran general says ready to help Iraq against militants," *Reuters*, June 29, 2014, http://www.reuters.com/article/2014/06/29/us-iraq-security-iran-idUSKBN0F407N20140629.

[13] Michael Eisenstadt and Jeffrey White, *An Enhanced Train-and-Equip Program for the Moderate Syrian Opposition: A Key Element of U.S. Policy For Syria and Iraq*, Washington Institute Policy Watch 2280, July 8, 2014, http://www.washingtoninstitute.org/policy-analysis/view/an-enhanced-train-and-equip-program-for-the-moderate-syrian-opposition; Chandler Atwood, Joshua Burgess, Michael Eisenstadt, and Joseph Wawro, *Between Not-In and All-In: U.S. Military Options in Syria*, Washington Institute Research Note No. 18, May 2014, http://www.washingtoninstitute.org/uploads/Documents/pubs/PolicyNote18_Atwood2.pdf.

Mr. POE. Thank you, gentlemen, and thank you all once again for your service, especially your military service.

I agree with you, General Keane, that it is futile to try to blame someone or someones for the situation that we find ourselves in today. That is not the issue. We are in a situation. Now, what does the United States do, if anything?

I agree with my friend from New York that this is a bigger event than a small civil war. It has been waged for centuries between Sunnis and Shi'as, and I see this as just more of the same that historically has had conflict in the region.

Assuming the United States backs off and watches what takes place, how is it going to play out? General, what do you think would play out? We just back off and we watch.

General KEANE. Yes. Well, first of all, you have to—it is convenient to characterize this as sectarian conflict a civil war. Shi'a and Sunni have been fighting each other for hundreds of years, and ISIL would love you to do that.

The fact of the matter is, the radical Islamist, the al-Qaeda movement, and now the ISIL movement, clearly wants to dominate all Arab lands—most of those are run by Sunnis—even though they are a Sunni-based terrorist organization.

So the fact is, if we sit back and do nothing, ISIL will continue to pursue its goals. I would agree about Iraq itself and Baghdad, it is likely they cannot succeed there, but it is not certain. They are skilled and crafty at what they do. They wouldn't launch an all-out attack on Baghdad. They go into Sunni neighborhoods, do what they did in 2006, conduct terrorist activities, and from there, own those neighborhoods and begin to mortar and rocket the Green Zone, et cetera, breaking will, suicide bombs going off, et cetera, making a run at the Green Zone as a limited attack to break will.

So ISIL, I don't think, is giving up. They are working around the periphery of Baghdad right now. We have been tracking it every single day. There are multiple attacks north, west, and south. So, clearly, they have a mind to go into Baghdad and be successful. I don't think they can be, but certainly I am telling you that is their objective.

The fact of the matter is, ISIL sitting there is very exposed to us. And if we accept the fact that they are a threat to the Middle East stability—and that seems blatantly obvious right now—and we have a 350 kilometer border with Syria that ISIL now owns, and there is a 175 kilometer border with Iraq that ISIL now owns, clearly, Jordan is next. They have stated it; it is next.

They are not going to go down the road to Jordan, like they did to Mosul. The Jordanian Air Force will blow them right off the road. But they will unite with the Salafists, bring foreign fighters in there, begin a major terrorist movement, use both borders with Jordan, that they own, and begin major infiltration. That is next. That is what is in front of us if we do nothing.

We have known sanctuary station bases, command and control facilities that are available to us to strike now. This is not about Sunni tribes. Sunni tribes are not in Syria. Sunni tribes are not up north where they are facilitating these operations from. They only are—they began to pick them up when they got into Mosul. There are plenty of targets that we have that we can start to do some damage to them.

Mr. POE. So you recommend air strikes?

General KEANE. Oh, yes. Sure. Absolutely.

Mr. POE. And what else?

General KEANE. Well, I would bring in our clandestine Special Operations Forces, let them pick the place they need to conduct operations, and start taking down ISIL leaders, high value targets, critical nodes that they can do. Those targets, believe me, after we have been applying all of our intelligence resources, just on what is going on in Mosul alone, are available to us now.

Mr. POE. All right. Thank you.

Just a couple more questions. Mr. Bandow, let me ask you two questions. What if it plays out to a three-state solution? As the Ambassador talked about earlier, the Kurds in the north and the two other provinces in the south, three states, is that such a bad idea?

Mr. BANDOW. A lot depends on specifically how it plays out. I don't think an independent Kurdistan is a bad idea. I think Turkey has come around with a willingness to deal, and I think that is very important. Until recently, that would have been quite problematic with Turkey.

The issue for the Sunni areas, of course, is oil and access to resources. Concern about Shi'a would be a Shi'a-dominated republic, would be under greater domination presumably of Iran. I think we are facing a situation of, compared to what? Can you hold the place together? Can you get a division that works out where you have some overall national government that is quite limited, and you have people at least willing, by separation, to live in peace.

I think nothing is going to come out of this easy, and nothing is going to come out of it without bloodshed. The question is, does a separation process like that give us a better chance to have a long-term peaceful solution as opposed to trying to hold it together. And my fear is we may have passed the point. Given the alienation of the Sunnis, can we hold it together at this point?

Mr. POE. All right. Thank you.

I will yield 5 minutes to the ranking member, Mr. Sherman from California.

Mr. SHERMAN. Thank you. At some point there will be peace. When that peace arrives, we may see an Iraq, Syria, and Lebanon that looks like Lebanon. That is to say, in Lebanon, you look at it on the map, it looks like one country. You go there and you have militias from the Druze, the Shi'ites, the Sunnis, and the Christians. We may go Syria and Iraq and see different areas controlled by the Alawites, Kurds, Sunnis, and Shi'ites.

One rhetorical question is: What if somebody in the Middle East threw a war and invited us and we didn't come? It wouldn't be necessarily the worst thing. I join with the chairman in thinking we need to look at our future policies rather than evaluate the past. I fear that—and I want to correct the record on this—that some of the opening statements seemed to be blinded by invective for the President that if we go down that road we are not going to reach good policy for the future.

And I think the gentleman from Arkansas, if I heard him correctly, said that the policy we have now is the worst possible policy we could possibly have. I would simply say that no American died in Iraq or Syria today, and there are many policies available to us which will cost us substantially in blood and treasure and will be counterproductive to our national security objectives.

We can perhaps improve the policy, but it starts not by claiming that the existing policy is the worst we could possibly have. Likewise, there were some who said that we had this great victory in Iraq that was recently squandered. We have Maliki. We had Iran domination or extreme influence. We had signed an agreement with Maliki to leave Iraq without a residual force, and we had an al-Maliki that was dead-set against signing any status of forces agreements that would have allowed us to leave a residual force.

And yet there are those who seem to think that only if the President had a different personality Maliki would be the Thomas Jefferson of Mesopotamia. I don't think that is the case.

As to oil, which is important in Iraq, the Sunnis are used to sharing more or less—they would argue less—their per capita share of substantial oil production. Now they have created a new state, or at least ISIS has, that leaves them with no—none of the Iraqi oil, and they do seem to control the Syrian oil.

Is anyone here able to tell me what this decline in—how great this decline in per capita oil revenues are and whether Sunnis can view themselves as having a future with so little per capita oil—or oil per capita?

General KEANE. The production in Syria is about 100,000 barrels at the most.

Mr. SHERMAN. So basically of the forces that control territory in the area—Kurd, Alawite, Sunni, and Shi'ite—it is the Islamic State that has by far the least oil per capita. That being the case, is this a future that Iraqi Shi'a and Sunnis can endorse?

General KEANE. They will start moving toward the other oil areas, I believe, Mr. Congressman, and that is part of their goal, to seize additional oil, for example, in the Kirkuk area, the Baiji refinery, and other things.

Mr. SHERMAN. Well, the refinery doesn't give you oil. Do you think that the Islamic State can defeat the Kurds in your Kirkuk?

General KEANE. They can't today, but they are going to be working on that.

Mr. SHERMAN. Anybody else have a different opinion? Mr. Eisenstadt?

Mr. EISENSTADT. If I could just add, basically, ISIL today is a parasitic and predatory organization. They don't have—as I mentioned in my testimony, maybe they were the richest terrorist group in the world; now they have to run the state, or at least they are claiming to run the state. And you need a lot more money to run a state than you do to run a terrorist organization.

It comes down to the government—their monthly budget or the annual budget is about $12 billion. So they don't have anywhere near that. So in order to get the money, they are going to have to find a way, you know, beyond, you know, preying on their own people, expanding their boundaries. And as a result, inherently their situation, first of all, creates opportunities for us, but it also creates dangers, because I think the logic of their situation will force them to expand vis-à-vis their neighbors in order to get oil.

Mr. SHERMAN. Let me ask one other question. I don't know if any of you has an answer. Iraq ran up $20 billion, $30 billion-plus of debt under Saddam Hussein, borrowing money to finance its war of aggression against Iran. Have they renounced that debt? Are they paying it, Ambassador Jeffrey?

Ambassador JEFFREY. Essentially, all of that debt was either paid off or forgiven, and they are in pretty good shape. They still have residual debts that pass through the U.N. to be paid to a compensation commission for Kuwait. But by and large, they are out of the red in that regard.

Mr. SHERMAN. And, finally, is there support for this Islamic State, substantial support, in either Jordan or Saudi Arabia, among the peoples there?

Mr. EISENSTADT. I have to—there was—the Saudis did announce I think in May that they arrested a cell of I think 52 people that they said was associated with ISIL. So there will be people throughout the region. They already have a presence in Lebanon. There are signs of sympathy in Jordan. So their message will resonate in certain sectors throughout the region, and that is why they are so dangerous.

General KEANE. Can I jump in on that? The Saudis and the Jordanians, as a state, believe that ISIL is a threat. Inside Saudi Arabia, as we have known for generations, there are sheikhs and other leaders who support Salafist movements and radical Islamist movements.

On the oil question that you asked, if you look at ISIL's objectives, they have no objectives to take the southern oil fields, nor even to attempt it. They leave that part of Iraq to Shi'a. It appears that they would have some interest in the northern oil fields. Just looking at their stated objectives, whether they can achieve that in the near term, I don't think so, but in the long term it is certainly a threat.

Mr. SHERMAN. Thank you.

Mr. POE. The Chair yields to the gentlelady from Florida, Ms. Ros-Lehtinen.

Ms. ROS-LEHTINEN. Thank you so much, Mr. Chairman.

Thank you, gentlemen, for excellent testimony. Constituents ask, what are our strategic goals and objectives in Iraq at the moment? Do you believe that the administration has formulated a rationale and a concrete policy for Iraq, or is it more of an ad hoc wait-and-see approach? That is my first question.

And President Obama said that the administration wouldn't fall into the trap of Whac-a-Mole foreign policy, and that ISIL is just one of a number of organizations that we have to stay focused on.

In his speech announcing that he was sending up to 300 advisors to Iraq, the President said that Iraqi leaders must come together around a political plan for Iraq's future, and that a Parliament should convene as soon as possible, yet we haven't really felt a sense of urgency from the administration to deal with ISIL or the political situation in Iraq yet.

Today, as we know, the Iraqi Government finally agreed on a new Sunni speaker, and they have 30 days to select a President, who will then task the majority party to form a government, so they can finally select a Prime Minister. How important do you think it is for Iraq to form a new inclusive government? And will that be enough to bring the people together? Or is it a case of too little too late and the damage has already been done by ISIL? And do you believe that Maliki needs to step aside in order to have any changes happen?

Ambassador, I will start with you.

Ambassador JEFFREY. Madam Chairman, first of all, last September at the U.N. the President laid out four goals that he would use all elements of national power to support in the Middle East—going after terrorist groups; supporting our partners an allies in the region, such as Jordan, such as Turkey, such as Iraq; working against weapons of mass destruction; and ensuring the free flow of oil.

Right now, three of those four are under pressure because of this development of ISIL—terrorist movement; friends and allies being threatened today and tomorrow, as my colleagues have talked about, with Jordan and Saudi Arabia; and, of course, eventually the free flow of oil, not because, as General Keane said, ISIL can move into the south.

What they can do is create enough chaos to put a damper on international engagement in the oil industry in the south. They can open the door for Iran to come in, and it is not in Iran's interest to have Iraq pumping more oil than Iran does, which——

Ms. ROS-LEHTINEN. Thank you, Mr. Ambassador.

Let me just go to the rest of the panel.

General KEANE. In reference to goals and objectives, certainly in the Middle East we want a stable and secure Middle East, and certainly we desired that for Iraq. And we wanted Iraq to be able to defend itself and not be a threat to its neighbors.

You know, the comment about the Whac-a-Mole, I think that is a really misguided comment, because the fact of the matter is radical Islam is on the rise in the Middle East. Obviously, we are focused on ISIL because of what they have accomplished, but it is on the rise in the Middle East and in Africa. And we have no comprehensive strategy to truly deal with that.

So it is not about whacking a mole. It is about using the region in a common strategy to work against this movement. It is an ideological movement, and we should come together, much as we did against Communist ideology, and unite together to do that, share in intelligence training partnerships, et cetera, and formalize those relationships. We are not doing that.

Ms. ROS-LEHTINEN. Thank you, sir.

Mr. Bandow.

Mr. BANDOW. Well, it would certainly appear to me that the administration desires both stability and unity when it comes to Iraq. The question of its policy and whether it is wait-and-see, it strikes me there is a certain prudential value in waiting and seeing in this case. That is, it is easier in, it is harder out once you are in, and especially without resolving the political situation in Baghdad.

It is hard for me to see a solution without getting a more inclusive government, and I have a hard time seeing that with Maliki. Whether that would be enough, I think it is going to be hard. It is going to require hard bargaining and showing the Sunnis, Shi 'ites, and their interest to share. That is, it is a tough road ahead.

Ms. ROS-LEHTINEN. Thank you.

Mr. Eisenstadt?

Mr. EISENSTADT. Two very quick points. The politics are key to the military's success. Politics got us to where we are, and in order to get ourselves out of this situation, the politics in Baghdad have to be right. So, yes, a broader, more representative government, is key.

Secondly, in terms of the administration's approach, I share their desire not to be sucked into a major military commitment in the region again. But if I was to critique on it, I would say that they tend to focus on solutionism. And they say we can't solve this problem with military means. And I would just say, yes, we can solve the region's problems, but that shouldn't be the criteria for assessing our intervention, because that still doesn't stop us from finding ways to shape region's dynamics in ways that advance our interests or stop worse things from happening.

Ms. ROS-LEHTINEN. Thank you very much. Thank you, gentlemen.

Thank you, Mr. Chairman.

Mr. POE. The Chair yields 5 minutes to the gentleman from Florida, Mr. Deutch.

Mr. DEUTCH. Thank you, Mr. Chairman. There has been a lot of talk about what ISIL is doing. I would just like to spend a minute talking about how they are doing it. There is a report that they gained some $400 million from the Mosul bank robbery. There were others who have suggested it might be closer to $60 million. How does that compare to the war chest of other terrorist groups? And what other entities and/or countries continue to support them financially? Any of you?

Mr. EISENSTADT. Yes. I mentioned before that they are predatory, and what I meant to say is that, although people focus on these spectacular bank heists, and the like, a lot of the money over the years has been as a result of extortion, shaking down people, both individuals and businesses, forcing people to pay taxes. The Christian communities have to pay a tax. They engage in smuggling of oil and weapons and antiquities. So a lot of this is pretty lucrative, but it is small change when you are talking about running a state.

Mr. DEUTCH. So there is any foreign entity that has any influence over that?

Mr. EISENSTADT. Well, there has been privately—been private investments from—excuse me, contributions from the Gulf, although that is probably—the Gulf States have been trying to clamp down on that as of late. But compared to what they earned domestically, they are self-sustaining as an entity based on what they are able to get from the Iraqis as well as from the oil transit trade, and stuff like that, and from the banks that they have been able to rob.

Mr. DEUTCH. All right. Thank you.

Thanks, Mr. Chairman. I yield back.

Mr. POE. The Chair recognizes the gentleman from Texas, Mr. Weber, for 5 minutes.

Mr. WEBER. Mr. Chairman, pass me up for the time being.

Mr. POE. The Chair recognizes the gentleman from Pennsylvania, Mr. Perry, for 5 minutes.

Mr. PERRY. Thank you, Mr. Chairman.

And thank you, gentlemen. Getting into I guess the finances and the structure of ISIS as a form of government—and I guess it is in some way across that territory governing the land it has taken— my curiosity is in the oil and the oil revenues and the transportation and the flow of the commodity itself. And I don't know which one of you is best to answer the question. Maybe everybody wants to weigh in.

But how is it that the transactions are taking place? First of all, how is the oil moving? Is it moving—is it being conducted through currently existing pipelines? And is it going to the coast? Is it going to other nation states?

Go ahead, Ambassador.

Ambassador JEFFREY. Again, ISIS has control over the fields in Syria that previously had up to 100,000 barrels a day. Not a huge amount, but still at $100 a barrel, even at smuggled prices, $50 or $25 a barrel, it generates a lot of money.

There are a number of fields in Iraq, small fields. Roughly, I have seen 10,000, 15,000 barrels that they are also getting back into operation, and that is yielding oil. There is a lot of stocked oil in Baiji that they could get their hands on. And, of course, if they can get the refinery, they can refine it, and it is a higher value.

There is no pipe—they have control of pipelines, but they can't use them. They are just blocking other people's use of them, including the central government or the Kurds. But what they are doing is participating in smuggling operations.

In my experience, many years in Turkey and in Iraq trying to track all of that is you have people involved in oil smuggling over the entire Middle East. It is a huge business. All kinds of people are involved. And once you get that kind of money flowing, literally, what you find is even enemies negotiate with each other on local deals to move oil and to move refined product around. It is extremely hard to stop, and we have seen this for, as I said, decades.

Mr. PERRY. So, Ambassador, is it moving by truck? It is not moving by rail.

Ambassador JEFFREY. No. Truck. Truck.

Mr. PERRY. All truck. So we are talking crude oil moved by truck.

Ambassador JEFFREY. Crude and refined products to the extent— because there are a lot of small refineries and quasi-refineries that people have developed along those areas.

Mr. PERRY. And what are they trading in? If they are selling it— it is my understanding in one report, selling it to Turkey. Syrian oil is sold to Turkey worth $800 million, and I am just curious about why Turkey would be buying oil from these folks.

Also, the Assad government potentially, but none of that makes sense to me, and it is essentially selling oil to the people that you are trying to depose.

Ambassador JEFFREY. It makes a lot of sense from my experience in the Middle East, Congressman, because people will sell oil to their enemies to get deals back. The Turkish Government isn't buying this oil, but middlemen, smugglers, gosh knows who in Turkey may be buying this.

I saw the $800 and $1,000 figure, and I thought it was a little bit high. But nothing would surprise me when it comes to truck smuggling in the Middle East, because every time I dismissed it or played it down I have been proven wrong.

Mr. PERRY. And what currency? Do they use one—do they use an Iraqi currency, or what currency are they using as a vehicle for fiduciary vehicle?

Ambassador JEFFREY. Everybody's favorite is dollars, Congressman, but people will use Iraqi, they will use Turkish, they will use Syrian.

Mr. PERRY. And is there any way to—I mean, that is financed through the operation, obviously. I mean, are they hoping to finance the operation? Is there any way from a financial standpoint—I imagine not based on—it sounds like the size of the operation, it is diverse enough and it is small enough that it would be pretty difficult to track it down. And it is not—probably doesn't have bank accounts associated with it. I am curious as to what our efforts are, if you know, and what they should be.

Ambassador JEFFREY. If we want to stop it, bomb the oil fields.

Mr. PERRY. Fair enough. Anybody else wish to comment? Is it— let me ask you this, with the world price of oil always in jeopardy and always of concern, at what point does it become important enough to do that? Because if we don't, they raise enough money to continue to grow what is not an Islamic group but an Islamic army, and fund it—at what point? Do we know?

Mr. BANDOW. I mean, that is obviously one way to try to defund them. Their biggest potential source of money would be oil as opposed to the other things that they do. And oil smuggling has always been big in the Middle East, and it is just very hard to stop.

Mr. PERRY. Thank you, Mr. Chairman. I yield.

Mr. POE. The Chair recognizes the gentleman from Illinois, Mr. Kinzinger.

Mr. KINZINGER. Thank you, Mr. Chair. Nothing like walking in and going right to questions.

Nice to see you all, and, again, thank you for all of your very hard work and your time spending with us and dealing with votes and everything.

As I mentioned in my opening statement, I think what we are seeing in Iraq right now is the worst-case scenario. Again, as somebody that was involved in fighting there, and somebody that saw firsthand the progress of the surge—I flew ISR aircraft, an RC–26—and watching the progress of the surge occur, when I went in 2008 and, you know, seeing a lot of attacks, and then in 2009 seeing people out playing on the streets and a relatively peaceful Iraq, to watch this fall apart has been very disheartening.

In fact, I think that—and I think we have to be very clear about the fact that a status of forces agreement was never really intended by this administration. If you want to see what the intention of a status of forces agreement is, look at what has happened in Afghanistan. The U.S. has not had that signed yet, but yet we continue to try to get that signed by the Afghan Government. Whereas, in Iraq we say, "Well, we tried and we just had to leave." And, again, what we are seeing is entirely predictable.

I hear a lot of people when we talk about Iraq say a couple of the following things. And this one offends me the most, but I hear some folks say, "Well, just let them all fight it out over there. Just let them deal with it over there." I also hear people say, "Well, if Iran and Russia are getting involved in Iraq, good; now they are going to get myred down in the problems we have seen in Iraq," which I would remind people that say that in fact Iran and Russia don't see being myred down quite like we do.

We see losing some troops, and every one we take very seriously and we hold precious, but we see that as being myred down. Whereas, Iran specifically does not see the loss of soldiers as any kind of being myred down. This is just what they do. They get involved in other countries' areas.

The other thing I have heard people say is that if a caliphate is established, well, the good news is at least now they are going to learn how hard it is to govern there. And I would also remind anybody that would say something like that that in fact they don't consider governing like we do. Governing to them is not building water towers and building roads and schools. Governing to them is ensuring that a guy is not walking down the street holding his girlfriend's hand, lest he lose his head. That is a very different way of doing things.

So what we are seeing there is the worst-case scenario. What I would like to do is just—I will start with the Ambassador and then go to the General, and if we have time work our way down. On some of the things I have mentioned about what people are saying for the reasons not to get involved—too complicated, you know, let them fight it out over there—what would be your reaction to that? Mr. Ambassador first.

Ambassador JEFFREY. First of all, I draw the line with live-scale combat troops on the ground. I want to make that clear, because I often advocate military force. But spending 4 years in Iraq and Vietnam, I am usually opposed to that unless I am very, very sure of the rationale.

But using other means of power, including everything that General Keane laid out in such great detail, I would be 100 percent in favor of that. The timing versus Maliki is important. But, no, we are not going to just sit back and watch these people just bash each other, because huge interests—the survival of Israel, the NATO borders in Turkey, the 20 percent of oil that flows out of the Gulf or global markets—all of these things are in play, and we need to be engaged or the situation is going to go even worse.

Who likes the situation we have seen now? As you pointed out, it is perhaps not the worst situation, because I could see it getting even worse, but this is about as bad as I think many of us have seen in the Middle East in a long, long time, and we need to act.

Mr. KINZINGER. Thank you. And, General, I will go to you in a second, but I do want to point out that we do want to see political solutions in Iraq. I would remind people that we had an Articles of Confederation in the United States, which we later threw out and adopted the Constitution of the United States to get it even more right.

But I don't think we can wait for this massive—this amazing political solution when Iraq, from a year ago, made multiple requests of the United States Government to take out these terrorist camps, and they were largely ignored.

General, what do you have to say to some of that?

General KEANE. Well, I have disagreed with the policy, because I—and I have had discussions with key administration officials about this. My own view is is that I do think we have to act, and I do think by acting it actually strengthens the political solution that we want as opposed to the reverse. And it gives us a much better seat at the table to have the kind of influence that we have had in the past.

And we absolutely have to bring our allies into the region here. They are eventually going to be threatened by this directly. They are now indirectly, and we should work with them. We should formulate a strategy together. But we are going to have to be the quarterback here. That is the reality.

Mr. KINZINGER. That is right. And let me—as I yield back, let me just say I get the politics of it. I believe, frankly, that the President withdrew from Iraq for political convenience. It would be much more politically convenient for me as a congressman that has to get elected to go back and say we are tired of every war in the Middle East and we just need to leave, but that is not what leadership is. And in 10 and 20 years, history is going to judge what we did with this moment. And I believe at this rate it is going to judge us very harshly.

And I yield back.

Mr. POE. The Chair recognizes the gentleman from Florida, Mr. DeSantis, for 5 minutes.

Mr. DESANTIS. Thank you, Mr. Chairman.

Thank the witnesses for your comments. I was really alarmed when the Iraqi army just melted in the face of ISIL. I mean, to say that they folded like a cheap suit is really an insult to cheap suits. It was pathetic. And I knew that there were problems when our forces left. I know it wasn't going to be easy. But we have invested a lot of time, money, and resources into training those individuals.

So, General Keane, I take from your testimony you think the reason or part of the reason that they folded like that was because of the politics coming out of the regime. Is that accurate?

General KEANE. Yes. He did much the same with the military as he did with his political opponents. You know, he sees this in the same rubric. You know, anybody that has done any time with Maliki, he is paranoid to a fault, insecure to a fault, and he is—you know, the art of politics for him is more about revenge than it is compromise. So that——

Mr. DESANTIS. Where does that leave us, though? I mean, it seems like you need to have a political solution in order to hope that we have an army there that can secure the country, which seems to me—I mean, it seems like that is going to be tough to ask for, at least in the near term.

General KEANE. Well, that is why I would like to get Ambassador Crocker and Petraeus over there to help, particularly on the military side. We know a lot of the leaders there, and the fact of the matter is they can be brought back. He pushed out the very distinguished leaders, battalion and brigade, and some extraordinary division commanders who distinguished themselves during the surge period in '07 and '08, and they were purged.

And these cronies came in, who none of the troops respected, and they were there long enough to truly break the cohesion in those organizations. And it is certainly sad for anybody that gave so much of their time to help grow an acceptable military, and I think that is what we had when we left. I mean, look at—they are not in our—we don't look at it through our prism or through a European military.

You have to look at it through the prism of what they are fighting, and they certainly met that, as far as we were concerned, in terms of meeting an acceptable challenge. But they are a mere shadow of their former self. It will be challenging to reconstruct it, as I said in my comments.

Mr. DeSANTIS. How do you—with respect to that, how do you see the role of Iran's Quds force? I know there have been reports that one of their leaders is in Baghdad participating or advising on operations. So is that just separate with, like, Shi'ite militia groups? Or is that Quds force now exercising control or influence with the actual remnants of the Iraqi army?

General KEANE. The Quds forces are providing advisors. There is no doubt about that. They are also very focused on the shrines in Samarra and also in Najaf and Karbala. I think they have probably received some pretty direct instructions not to let those shrines fall into ISIL's hands.

But the fact of the matter is, Iran has an influence here. And I think, as we sit on our hands and not do much about anything, that influence will grow. Their seat at the table will grow in stature, because Maliki is making a case right now. You can just hear him saying it, "Look at, I have got international support. I have got the—I have got Iran here, and I have got the Russians here." Both of them want him to stay in power.

And, really, everybody at this table, and anyone who knows anything about this situation, knows that he has to go or we are never going to get to some kind of a coalition government. The fact of the matter is that we cannot let that influence continue to grow and fester, or we will never be able to get to a better government solution than what we have.

Mr. DeSANTIS. In terms of—and this is any—and I would like to get everyone's thought on this. I think you made a good point, General, when you said that it is not just sectarian. There are sectarian conflicts, but ISIS's goal is to topple Sunni regimes in the region. As I look at it, it seems to me that Jordan would be maybe one of the first ones that would be in their line of sight.

So what is the panelists' view on which regimes specifically that we are allied with would be the most vulnerable? Is it the Hashemite Kingdom of Jordan? And we will start with the Ambassador and go down the line.

Ambassador JEFFREY. It is Iraq itself. It is the Kurdish areas of the north. Eventually, if these guys build up more steam, then it is Jordan. But eventually it is the Gulf States. That is their target is to move into that area with its incredible riches.

General KEANE. I agree with that.

Mr. BANDOW. Yes. Certainly, Jordan is very vulnerable. I mean, it has a competent military, but its social circumstances—refugees, economic position, kind of the impact of the Arab Spring and discontent that it has—all of that makes it very vulnerable.

Mr. EISENSTADT. All I will just say is that it may depend on circumstances and where they perceive an opportunity, but this is all the more reason why we need to put pressure on them in Syria and Iraq, so that they don't feel that they have the luxury of being able to engage in adventurism, you know, that they have to focus on just defending their position in Syria and Iraq, so they can't engage in that.

Mr. DESANTIS. Great. Mr. Chairman, thank you for holding this hearing. And I am concerned, and I know the chair is, about people with Western passports, Americans who are now fighting over there. They cannot be allowed, obviously, to come back in the United States and wage war against us here.

And I yield back.

Mr. POE. The Chair recognizes the gentleman from Texas.

Mr. WEBER. Thank you, Mr. Chair.

General Keane, some of the reading that I read said that the ISL really did not have easily discernible targets. So you are talking about doing air strikes and knocking out much of their capability. That seems contradictory.

Are we able to go after them if the President—and let me just say, first, it seems like the President all of a sudden is against the withdrawal. Now, before he was for the withdrawal, before he was against the withdrawal. Are you all getting that sense out of the White House? He might wish he had left some forces there?

General KEANE. I can't speak for the White House, Mr. Congressman. But the fact of the matter is there are targets available to us. If you are dealing around the highly populated areas in Baghdad where we are having contested fights, our ability to distinguish between Sunni tribes and ISIL is probably next to nothing.

So that would be a challenge. The only way we would be able to facilitate that use of airpower is where air-ground controllers are in a fight and they know who they are in with and they can target them.

But let us put that aside. The fact of the matter is, ISIL began this movement out of sanctuaries and staging bases in Syria. They are still there. They have lines of communication that are vulnerable there. They are moving equipment back and forth. Those are available targets to us.

Up north, where this is no longer a contested area, there are staging bases and sanctuaries there that are available to us. This is air interdiction. ISIL identifies the target, and we strike——

Mr. WEBER. Okay. So you are talking about going back to their bases and working your way back towards——

General KEANE. Listen, this wouldn't be like an air campaign we did in Afghanistan and Iraq where we had hundreds of sorties a day. It wouldn't even be anything like what the Israelis are doing with Hamas at 80 sorties a day. This is selected and limited use of air power.

Mr. WEBER. Let me move on. Ambassador, if you could be President for a day, would you go ahead and bomb those oil fields?

Ambassador JEFFREY. I might do that eventually, but I would have some better targets. As the General said, at this point, before the political situation coalesces, I would pick a few targets where we can definitely, through our drones and intelligence, identify ISIS and basically show that this administration is willing to use force against what is essentially an al-Qaeda element in Iraq when we are striking al-Qaeda all over the rest of the Middle East.

Mr. WEBER. Is that a preclusion to becoming—I think the General said the quarterback bringing in our allies, saying that we are willing to do this?

Ambassador JEFFREY. At this point, limited military force would be a leverage factor, a multiplier of our influence, because right now this will make all the difference and people are wondering whether we are going to do it.

Mr. WEBER. You also said—let me ask you this, and I will ask this of the whole panel. What are the chances of ISIS, ISIL, call them whatever, once they establish this state, assuming—and let us just say for argument's sake they are successful—do they then turn on Syria?

Ambassador JEFFREY. Eventually, they turn on everybody. That is what we have seen with al-Qaeda movements——

Mr. WEBER. Okay.

Ambassador JEFFREY [continuing]. As they get real strong.

Mr. WEBER. General Keane?

General KEANE. Our analysts believe over at ISW and, you know, what they are tracking, is clearly Jordan is next, but—and then they would go west into Syria, toward Damascus would be the——

Mr. WEBER. Mr. Bandow?

General KEANE. Right. Exactly.

Mr. BANDOW. Yes. Their expressed ambitions are quite wide, so I would expect Syria and Jordan to be on their list.

Mr. WEBER. Mr. Eisenstadt, do you want to round out the foursome?

Mr. EISENSTADT. Yes. I will just say that, again, it may be that they will start off with a plan to do Jordan first, and then move on to Lebanon. But, again, it depends where they have the most opportunity I think.

Mr. WEBER. Okay. And then, General Keane, you said Maliki was paranoid to a fault. I think that was you. I mean, can you blame him? Number one. But, number—I guess more appropriately, who do you bring in in that situation that is not paranoid in that situation? Who is his successor?

General KEANE. Well, there is no doubt of the fact that there was a leadership train in Iraq, and the choices were few. And then, if you reflect back to that first election, it was a question of, you know, who could people agree with? And nobody's number one or two was even close to being selected. So, by default, we got Maliki.

I think the tragedy of Maliki is when we had the opportunity to get a different government, the second—in the second election, when he actually lost by one vote, we had made that decision then, the year before, to politically disengage from the Maliki government.

This was an administration decision made in 2009, and by that time we were well into our hands off of shaping the political future of Iraq, which I have always thought was a mistake because we did that to great success in Germany, Italy, Japan, South Korea, Philippines, Bosnia-Herzegovina, doing that very thing because of the stake in our own interest and the sacrifices that had been made.

Mr. WEBER. Thank you, Mr. Chairman. I thank you.

Mr. POE. The gentleman yields back? I assume he does.

One question, General Keane. Saudi Arabia is in the middle of this. Why aren't they doing something?

General KEANE. Well, my experience with this is when they feel the threat, their intelligence services are on it. They are not as good as the Jordanian intelligence service, to be sure, but they need to be led. And that would be first step for me is meet with allies, let us share intelligence, let us identify what this is, what is the approach to deal with this, et cetera. And who can contribute to doing it.

And I think that is the only way to approach this problem, that we should—but we need to lead it, to answer your question, Mr. Chairman. They are not going to do anything unilaterally unless their territory, their sovereignty is violated. But they have much to offer here in taking a collective response to what is taking place.

And I am not just speaking militarily. I am also speaking diplomatically and politically in assisting what needs to take place.

Mr. POE. All right. Thank you.

The Chair yields 5 minutes to the gentleman from Illinois, Mr. Schneider.

Mr. SCHNEIDER. Thank you, Chairman Poe.

And, again, thank you to the witnesses for your testimony and your insights today. I think, General Keane, you may have said something very poignant—it is the tragedy of Maliki. And I think history may look on this as one of the key aspects of where we are today.

But let me start with Ambassador Jeffrey. You talked in your written testimony about Plan A, and the objective of a unified Iraq. I will open this to the whole panel. Why is it so crucial to maintain a unified Iraq?

Ambassador JEFFREY. First of all, if one of the states in the Middle East starts to unravel, the risk is, as we saw in the Balkans in the 1990s, that other states start unraveling or other states start trying to pick up the pieces. And in the Middle East there are five juicier pieces than in the Balkans because of the oil, because of the history of weapons of mass destruction, and the potential for countries to develop it again.

Syria tried it a few years ago in a nuclear account. Iraq's history, we all know, and we know the situation with Iran. So you have got tremendous built-up tensions that would explode if the place fell apart. Iran would gain power by dominating the oil fields to the south. The al-Qaeda movement worldwide would gain power. And America's role as the defender of states with whom we have had very strong security relationships—in this case the ex-state of Iraq—would be down the toilet. And I just don't see that as a good scenario.

Mr. SCHNEIDER. I appreciate that. The distinction—one distinction I see is that in the Balkans you had historic geographic nation states. The nation states in this region historically, you know, Iran with the Persian history, Turkey, Ottoman, Egypt. But the others are a creation of 1916. How do we keep that together?

Ambassador JEFFREY. I have spent almost as much of my career in the Balkans as in the Middle East, and the two areas in some respects are very similar. Once you start redrawing boundaries, it never stops, Congressman.

Mr. SCHNEIDER. I understand.

Ambassador JEFFREY. It doesn't stop in Germany. It doesn't stop anywhere.

Mr. SCHNEIDER. I understand. And you said later in your testimony that the Kurds have to be brought in to the Iraqi camp. You know, they have taken steps to pull further away. Is it possible even to bring them back, even if Maliki is——

Ambassador JEFFREY. Oh, I think so. Their deal right now is 17 percent of all Iraqi oil exports. Under the right arrangements when they were negotiated in December, that would get them up to about $13 billion or $14 billion a year. You go to the Kurdish areas, you go to Irville now, and you see a booming area, the likes of which you would see nowhere else in the Middle East other than along the Gulf and in Israel. And that is thanks to the proceeds from the rest of—from the oil pump basically in the south.

Mr. SCHNEIDER. Right.

Ambassador JEFFREY. They will have oil. They have oil in their own areas, and they have some oil now in Kirkuk. They can export that if they go independent, but they won't have the same earnings and they are going to be in a militarily much more difficult situation, because they will be on their own facing ISIS. Thus, they have had to mobilize their reserves.

They have 100,000 reserves. Many of them are under arms now. It is not a good economic financial situation, totally apart from the fact Iran is violently opposed—and I underline "violently opposed"—to them becoming independent for several other reasons.

Under the right leadership in Baghdad—and that means no Maliki—I think they could be brought back in.

Mr. SCHNEIDER. If Maliki stays, is that an option?

Ambassador JEFFREY. If Maliki goes.

Mr. SCHNEIDER. No. But what if he stays?

Ambassador JEFFREY. If he stays, they are never coming back.

Mr. SCHNEIDER. Okay. Then, the thing starts.

General Keane, let me turn to you. You had talked about the need to defeat ISIS, ISIL, Islamic State, whatever we are calling it, as well as the need to defeat radical Islam. Can there be a distinction drawn between successfully defeating ISIL and defeating radical Islam in general?

General KEANE. You are suggesting—is that a worthy goal?

Mr. SCHNEIDER. No, not as a worthy goal. Radical Islam is a much—is much broader than strictly the geography that ISIS is focused on. The need—clearly, we have to defeat ISIS. Can we defeat ISIS now without defeating radical Islam now? Or is there steps——

General KEANE. Well, I have always believed that we have needed a comprehensive strategy to deal with this ideology for some time. And much as we formed political or military alliances to deal with the Communist ideology, most of which were successful, we should be pursuing those same kind of alliances to share common political beliefs, intelligence training, et cetera.

This is not about U.S. leading the efforts in African countries. This is about a shared responsibility, and we assist them so that they can function adequately themselves. And I think one of the things that happened to us, after we got so focused on the senior leadership in al-Qaeda, and which we have truly done damage to them, we took away everything that they really wanted, and we should feel good about that.

But being so possessed by that, we neglected the spread of radical Islam which has really taken place. And we really don't have much of a strategy to deal with it. In fact, it was difficult for the administration at first even to admit it, and now finally they are beginning to admit it, but we still need a strategy to cope with it.

And ISIL—the speed of what they have achieved certainly has now got our attention, and we are going to do something about it. And I just keep raising my hand once in a while to—even that is important to us. It is a top priority. But we need a broader strategy than what ISIL——

Mr. SCHNEIDER. I agree. It has to be everything.

I know I am out of time. Mr. Eisenstadt, you looked like you wanted to say something, but I—Mr. Chairman, thank you. There are so many more questions. I appreciate the time you have given us today, and I look forward to hearing more.

Mr. POE. Thank you, gentlemen. Thank all four of you for being here today. The information has been very valuable.

The subcommittees are adjourned. Thank you once again.

[Whereupon, at 4:24 p.m., the subcommittees were adjourned.]

APPENDIX

MATERIAL SUBMITTED FOR THE RECORD

JOINT SUBCOMMITTEE HEARING NOTICE
COMMITTEE ON FOREIGN AFFAIRS
U.S. HOUSE OF REPRESENTATIVES
WASHINGTON, DC 20515-6128

Subcommittee on Terrorism, Nonproliferation, and Trade
Ted Poe (R-TX), Chairman

Subcommittee on the Middle East and North Africa
Ileana Ros-Lehtinen (R-FL), Chairman

TO: MEMBERS OF THE COMMITTEE ON FOREIGN AFFAIRS

You are respectfully requested to attend an OPEN hearing of the Committee on Foreign Affairs, to be held jointly by the Subcommittee on Terrorism, Nonproliferation, and Trade and the Subcommittee on the Middle East and North Africa in Room 2172 of the Rayburn House Office Building (and available live on the Committee website at http://www.ForeignAffairs.house.gov):

DATE: Tuesday, July 15, 2014

TIME: 2:00 p.m.

SUBJECT: The Rise of ISIL: Iraq and Beyond

WITNESSES: The Honorable James Jeffrey
Philip Solondz Distinguished Visiting Fellow
The Washington Institute for Near East Policy
(Former U.S. Ambassador to Iraq)

General Jack Keane, USA, Retired
Chairman of the Board
Institute for the Study of War

Mr. Doug Bandow
Senior Fellow
Cato Institute

Mr. Michael Eisenstadt
Senior Fellow and Director of the Military and Security Studies Program
The Washington Institute for Near East Policy

By Direction of the Chairman

The Committee on Foreign Affairs seeks to make its facilities accessible to persons with disabilities. If you are in need of special accommodations, please call 202/225-5021 at least four business days in advance of the event, whenever practicable. Questions with regard to special accommodations in general (including availability of Committee materials in alternative formats and assistive listening devices) may be directed to the Committee.

COMMITTEE ON FOREIGN AFFAIRS

MINUTES OF SUBCOMMITTEE ON *Terrorism Nonproliferation and Trade; Middle East and North Africa* HEARING

Day __*Tuesday*__ Date____ *July 15, 2014* ____ Room_____ *2172* _____

Starting Time __*2:00 p.m.*__ Ending Time __*4:24 p.m.*__

Recesses __*1*__ (*2:30* to *3:12*) (___to____) (___to____) (___to____) (___to____) (___to____)

Presiding Member(s)

Chairman Ted Poe

Check all of the following that apply:

Open Session ☑
Executive (closed) Session ☐
Televised ☑

Electronically Recorded (taped) ☑
Stenographic Record ☑

TITLE OF HEARING:

"The Rise of ISIL: Iraq and Beyond"

SUBCOMMITTEE MEMBERS PRESENT:

Reps. Poe, Ros-Lehtinen, Chabot, Kinzinger, Cotton, Weber, Perry, DeSantis, Meadows, Yoho, Sherman, Deutch, Connolly, Higgins, Cicilline, Vargas, Schneider, Kennedy

---

NON-SUBCOMMITTEE MEMBERS PRESENT: *(Mark with an * if they are not members of full committee.)*

HEARING WITNESSES: Same as meeting notice attached? Yes ☑ No ☐
(If "no", please list below and include title, agency, department, or organization.)

STATEMENTS FOR THE RECORD: *(List any statements submitted for the record.)*

QFR - Rep. Kennedy
Statement for the Record - Rep. Connolly

TIME SCHEDULED TO RECONVENE _____
or
TIME ADJOURNED __*4:24 p.m.*__

Subcommittee Staff Director

Statement for the Record
Submitted by Mr. Connolly of Virginia

The United States faces no good options in Iraq. And those today who place blame for Iraq's current crisis at President Obama's doorstep conveniently ignore the facts on the ground and their own complicity in support of the 2003 invasion that was ill conceived, lacked any Plan B and failed to reconstruct a post-Saddam nation. To understand the rise of the Islamic State of Iraq and the Levant (ISIL), we must first consider the landscape that proved fertile ground for this brutal and insidious terrorist organization. In other words, our necessary context is the legacy of the 2003 Iraq War. This context is instructive for how ISIL has become an ascendant terrorist organization and why our options for addressing this growing source of regional instability are limited. Further, the failure of the Iraqi government to govern effectively and responsibly has deprived the U.S. of a reliable partner in the effort to defeat ISIL and prevent the group's proliferation.

The lineage of ISIL can be traced to Al-Qaeda in Iraq (AQI), a vicious organization founded in the wake of the destruction of the Iraq War and headed by Abu Musab al-Zarqawi. The organization was infamous for indiscriminate attacks on civilians, beheadings, and kidnappings. It was out of AQI that the Islamic State of Iraq, later to be known as ISIL, was formed by Abu Bakr al-Baghdadi. The radical movement has since spread to Syria and most recently launched several sweeping offensives in Iraq that have moved from Mosul to Tikrit, Tel Afar, Baqubah, and Haditha.

It is an offensive that ISIL conducted earlier this year that provides insight into the difficult choice that faces the U.S. in deciding the course of action in Iraq. In January 2014, ISIL forces gained control of the city of Fallujah, the site of building-to-building combat in 2004 that resulted in more than 100 fallen American soldiers and over 1,000 casualties. Despite the significant sacrifice made by American forces in 2004, the decision whether or not to return to Iraq in 2014 to regain control of the hard-won city was not a clear one and one that this Committee wrestled with in a February 2014 hearing entitled, "Al–Qaeda's Resurgence in Iraq: A Threat to U.S. Interests."

General Jack Keane, one of our distinguished witnesses for today's hearing, co-authored a June 2014 Op-Ed in the Wall Street Journal that outlined a military package for Iraq that included intelligence architecture, military planners and advisers, special operations forces, and U.S. air power. General Keane argued that this would help turn the tide against the ISIL onslaught, and prefaced the outline with the following statement: "Setting aside for the moment the question of whether this administration has the will to intervene again in Iraq, here are the components of a reasonable military package that can make a difference."

I am afraid this preface misses the point about where the willingness to intervene, or lack thereof, is being derived. It is the American people who are understandably wary of another intervention in Iraq. A recent Quinnipiac University poll found that American voters oppose 63 - 29 percent sending U.S. ground troops back into Iraq, and when asked about air strike options, a plurality, or 39%, would prefer that the U.S. not conduct air strikes. After 9 years of a deeply unpopular war and 4,486 American soldiers killed, there is a very limited appetite among the American public to commit additional soldiers and resources to the crisis we are witnessing in Iraq. That is true whether you think the U.S. should intervene or not.

Further hindering the ability of the U.S. to intervene and take effective action in Iraq is the government led by Prime Minister Nouri al-Maliki. After Prime Minister Maliki refused to grant U.S. troops legal immunity and the subsequent departure of U.S. forces in 2011, Maliki purged the government and military of effective leaders along sectarian lines that favored fealty over competence. Not surprisingly, this bred resentment among disaffected Sunni populations. An Iraqi government that cannot reach out to moderate minority populations, much as U.S. forces did to turn the tide in Iraq, will prove to be a counterproductive partner. Unfortunately, Iraq's legislature failed to take a step forward on Sunday when it suspended proceedings without naming a new speaker of the parliament, president and prime minister.

I hope our witnesses today can shed further light on the context in which ISIL has expanded its reach and resources. Organizations that breed violence and terror are not created in a vacuum. I believe this context will not only help us understand the origins of ISIL but where it may seek to continue its expansion.

Questions for the Record
Submitted by the Honorable Joseph Kennedy
To General Keane

Question 1:

General Keane, thank you for your testimony and for your service to our nation. As I look over your statement, particularly your suggestions for possible U.S. action in the region, I am reminded of the cost to the United States, both in resources and lives lost, during the Iraq War and in previous conflicts in the Middle East. While ensuring the security of the U.S. and our allies must remain at the top of the priority list, we also must weigh the short- and long-term impact of our decisions.

In your testimony you state, "ISIL can be effectively attacked in Syria and Iraq using air power to destroy known sanctuaries, staging bases, lines of communication and command and control facilities." Additionally, you state, "Special operation forces should be clandestinely employed to attack high value targets particularly in Iraq but eventually expanded into Syria."

If the US were to launch air attacks and dispatch to Iraq a team lead by Ambassador Crocker and General Petraeus, as you suggest, how many U.S. troops or personnel would be needed? How long would they be deployed and can you estimate the costs associated with this type of U.S. engagement?

Question 2:

There is large consensus that Iraq must have the political will to overcome ISIL and establish an inclusive government in order for a more durable peace to take hold. What suggestions do you have, beyond military tactics, to achieve this goal, to create an environment that is receptive to political change?

[NOTE: Responses were not received to the preceding questions prior to printing.]